Why didn't anyone tell me that?

Beyond the psychiatric textbook

Why didn't anyone tell me that?
Beyond the psychiatric textbook:
What they don't teach the psychiatric trainee

Robert M Cohen

Quay Books
MA Healthcare Limited

Quay Books Division, MA Healthcare Limited, Jesses Farm, Snow Hill, Dinton, Salisbury, Wiltshire, SP3 5HN

British Library Cataloguing-in-Publication Data
A catalogue record is available for this book

© Robert Cohen 2004
ISBN 1 85642 279 8

Printed in the UK by Cromwell Press, Trowbridge

Contents

Introduction

If you watch any of the numerous medical dramas on TV, you will be transported to an age when doctors were well-respected pillars of the community, often passing their knowledge, wisdom and business to their sons. Set in a pretty country location, life seems idyllic.

If this picture was ever true, it certainly is not the case now. Advances in knowledge, ever increasing demands on limited resources, and changes in society's attitude to the medical profession, mean that the picture today is very different.

My own experience, shared by numerous medical colleagues, is that the care and treatment of patients with a variety of medical disorders is one of the most satisfying jobs you can possibly have. And the specialty of psychiatry, which deals with illnesses that strike at the heart of what it is to be a human being, is truly awesome.

But since qualifying as a doctor and going up the ladder to being a consultant, I have had to learn a great number of things that have been necessary to allow me to work as a doctor in my chosen field, even though they are not, strictly speaking, about the practice of medicine, but rather about the world of work.

The characters in idyllic TV dramas do not have the sort of problems that occur in real life (apart from the numerous affairs and indiscretions that seem now to be a feature of almost any drama, whatever the setting). They do not have doctors with career problems, struggling how to choose what discipline to undertake. They do not have doctors coping with higher training; balancing their work life with a variety of domestic responsibilities; working with multidisciplinary teams; being expected to do more with an ever-diminishing set of resources; and being micromanaged and constantly assessed. Perhaps the medical profession in the real world has also been slow to wake up fully to the impact of the new world in which we work. So, if you are a recently qualified doctor, there are few structures in place to help you and guide you through your career.

In a variety of ways — perhaps assisting a surgeon in the operating theatre, or drinking tea in sister's office after a medical ward round, or going on a community visit with a psychiatrist or a GP — you may have had the opportunity to gain brief individual pieces of more personal career advice from a senior colleague. One of the striking features of the medical profession is the willingness of senior staff in a variety of situations to offer help to their junior colleagues, even in brief professional encounters. But even if, in the course of several years, you get a number of pieces of advice from many senior colleagues, you still have to put it together yourself.

One structural feature that has been instituted over the last twenty years that is invaluable is 'supervision'. This refers to the situation where a senior colleague, usually the consultant, sits with a junior colleague for an hour a week to discuss any problems that the junior colleague is having with his or her professional duties in the current post. Originally a demand from the Royal Colleges as a condition of approval of training posts, it is now the NHS that is requiring its senior staff to offer supervision to the junior staff — to whom the consultant is now the line manager. But the implementation of supervision is patchy.

As well as discussing cases that might be troubling the junior doctor, supervision provides the trainee with the opportunity to raise a number of issues that might be interfering with the ability to fulfil the needs of the job. Some may be directly related to the job itself – such as clarifying which tasks are the responsibility of the post-holder, and which are not; or how to give a presentation at the case conference coming up next week. Others are external, such as how to approach the MRCPsych examination; or how to cope with strong feelings arising from the loss of a parent and still ensure that, with the mind of the bereaved not fully concentrating on work, the job is done to a satisfactory standard.

A senior doctor can only give guidance in these situations. A consultant cannot treat a doctor in his or her own firm; a doctor cannot give formal bereavement counselling or even support the junior through it. But it is possible to make some general comments that can still make a big difference.

This book tries to offer a series of such guiding comments for doctors who are thinking of, or who have embarked on, a training in psychiatry in the UK. It offers some thoughts on how you might approach making the decision whether to try out psychiatry. It offers you some general comments about how you can find a training programme (and both Senior House Officer and Specialist Registrar level) and how you can get the best out of such a training programme. It considers a number of practical matters that may be going on in your life outside work. It introduces some aspects of management skills that you will need in the modern working environment. And it considers the political environment in which you will be working — to help you understand why certain apparent absurdities in health care are why they are. In the course of a training, you will almost certainly not be able to change anything (unless you become a medical politician on the side), but the information may help you to live with what you cannot change.

You might wonder if all this is really necessary. I can only say that in the course of supervising many doctors at SHO, SpR, staff grade and associate specialist grades, all the issues in this book — and more — have come up at one time or other. I have advised them, as I advise you now, that I am not an 'expert' on many of these matters and that my comments should be seen as no more than 'common sense'-type comments. Nevertheless, they have given my colleagues enough to start the process of solving their problems. When they needed formal advice — financial, legal, emotional or other — they have gone to suitably qualified professionals. You should bear this in mind and take steps to seek proper professional advice when you need it.

But with the information in this book, you will be better equipped to deal with the challenges that occur in the course of a training in psychiatry that do not relate to the direct provision of clinical care. And as such, I hope you will be able to get as much enjoyment from learning about a most fascinating discipline as I did.

Good luck!

Robert M Cohen
March 2004

1

Planning a career

So. You are thinking of a career in psychiatry? Maybe you have just completed your house year and are looking to start as a fully registered doctor with something that involves more talking to people than general surgery. Or you are a GP trainee who has noticed the psychosocial aspects of patient care. Or you are a medical student and you have some idea of treating 'the whole person'. Or you are at some other stage in your life or career and are just curious. Whatever your reason for thinking about psychiatry: welcome.

To decide whether or not you want to do something, you need some idea of what you are letting yourself in for. So let's start by thinking about what psychiatry is. Or rather, what it is not. Many people, including many who should know better, think that psychiatry is some sort of dustbin for doctors (and you do have to be medically qualified to be a psychiatrist) who can't do anything else; for doctors who like to be nice to people; for doctors who like to chat to people without really doing much.

But psychiatry is no such thing: it is a serious medical discipline, with a great deal of knowledge being applied to a particular group of disorders affecting the mind. The knowledge helps us to recognise these disorders and to alleviate their effects. As with any other medical disorder, there are some conditions we can cure. More frequently, there are some in which we can reduce the harm they cause. Occasionally, when there is no medical intervention, we can still provide comfort and support. And psychiatrists are still subject to the dictum *primum non nocere* — 'the first thing is not to do any harm'. From time to time, a non-expert doctor kills a patient by ignoring textbook psychiatric advice; or a relative or friend inadvertently contributes to the demise of a loved one. And even if the patient does not die, injudicious treatment can prolong a difficult situation. But do not think that this means that the inexpert doctor or the unaware person is to be blamed. What I am trying to convey is that there is a body of specialist knowledge and expertise that psychiatrists have. As well as clinical experience of patients, this expertise comes from a wide range of scientific — and, at times, artistic — disciplines. If you want to be a psychiatrist, you have to gain clinical experience and learn a good deal of research-based information.

An overview of the scope of psychiatry is detailed in *Figure 1.1*. It is a classification that fits with clinical experience. The World Health Organization produces an *International Classification of Diseases*, in which the tenth edition has a chapter dedicated to Mental Disorder (WHO, 1995). The American Psychiatric Association produces a *Diagnostic and Statistical Manual*, which is in its fourth edition (DSM-IV; APA 1995).

Psychiatric disorder can be divided into psychosis and neurosis. In lay terms, psychotic disorders are those in which the patient's mental presentation is different from their typical one. When ill, the patient sometimes seems almost to be a different person to the person they are when they are well. For example, a patient with schizophrenia (a psychotic disorder) may hold a belief that he is Jesus Christ when ill, which he does not hold when he is well. But a patient with a neurotic disorder will seem to be the same person. With a disorder such as obsessive-compulsive disorder (a neurotic disorder), a person may feel a constant intrusive thought of a swear word, such as 'shit', but that person will recognise at the time that the symptom is abnormal and will complain about it.

It is an important clinical distinction, in that it will affect the way that the clinician talks to the patient. Talk is a crucial clinical tool, undervalued by those who are impressed only by expensive technology. Using the right language can help prevent someone committing suicide; defuse a potentially violent situation; and help an entrenched patient move in a more helpful direction. Although some people are instinctively more attuned than others to the language they should use with patients in any given clinical situation, it should be borne in mind that language skills can be taught.

But the selection of this distinction, between psychosis and neurosis, is only one aspect of the differences between illnesses, and the research classifications do not favour it. Years ago, it may have represented a distinction between 'biological' illnesses (psychotic) and 'psychological' illnesses (neurotic), with the implication that biological illnesses were real illnesses and psychological illnesses were not (preserved in the disparaging phrase, 'it's all in the mind'). Things have moved on significantly since those days, and our understanding of the conditions is significantly advanced.

Illnesses such as the dementias have always been seen as 'genuine', because reseachers have recognised that the brain is heavily involved in the mental functions, and damage to the brain as a result of identifiable physical illness causes a number of syndromes. Acute damage, such as overwhelming liver failure or a serious blow to the brain from a punch, can cause someone to lose consciousness or become acutely confused. In such circumstances, treatment of the medical condition that causes the confusion may lead to a resolution of the mental problem and the person may return to normal. But the brain does not always recover from damage, and there may be some loss of previous function. The term 'dementia' means the loss of a function that the brain previously had – such as the loss of the ability to speak, or to calculate where the mouth is in relation to the spoon while eating. This is in contrast to the term mental handicap (the present politically correct term is 'learning disabilities', though this does not cover the true extent of many patients' impairments), in which the brain fails to develop functions that it should.

People are less sympathetic about changes in the mental state as a result of acute intoxication. Somebody who is drunk is often seen as responsible for choosing to become intoxicated and therefore responsible for their actions. Others disagree, believing that people should be excused actions committed when intoxicated. Medicine is morally neutral. It is not the job of the doctor to apportion blame – simply to recognise the processes that occur and describe them. Doctors, like other members of the community, are entitled to hold personal views relating to personal conduct and morality. However, they are not entitled to make moral judgements. For example, a doctor may not approve of sexual promiscuity, but it is not appropriate for such a doctor to refuse to treat someone for a dementing condition on the basis that the infection causing the mental disorder was acquired through sexual contact outside marriage.

What is interesting about psychiatry, unlike other branches of medicine, is that the relationship between mental disorder and socially unacceptable behaviours is complex. Psychiatrists are often asked to advise the law courts, and teasing out the various strands of argument can be very complicated. For example, it is the opinion of this author, who has a specialist expertise in the treatment of addiction, that one of the facets of the addiction is that it is a disorder of the psychological function of responsibility. Addicts often do not take responsibility for themselves or their actions. It is anticipated that a biological basis for this, possibly in the structure of the frontal lobe, will be found in the not-too-distant future. Now, it may therefore be argued that, since addiction is a recognised medical condition and part of the medical condition is a disorder of responsibility, all addicts should be excused any anti-social action and therefore not convicted of any crime they may commit. An analogy is that a person with influenza should be excused of work while ill – the current concept of the 'sick role'.

However, this argument would itself be defeated by the inadequacy of the understanding of the psychological function of responsibility, which develops in response to previous experiences of losing things as a consequence of the original action. No doubt, in time, this will also be shown to have a biological correlate that changes with status.

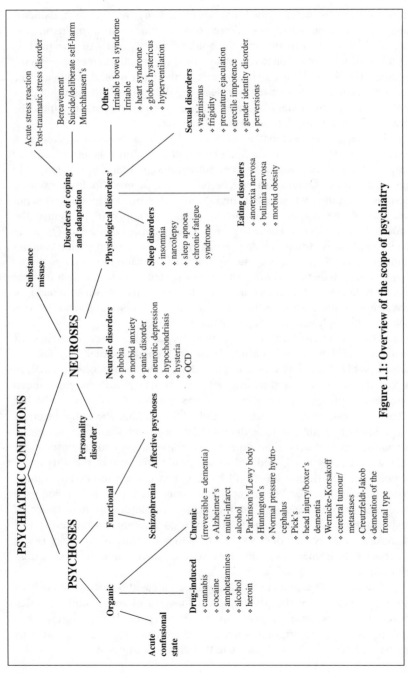

Figure 1.1: Overview of the scope of psychiatry

The implication is that, rather than let off addicts of any crime committed as addicts, the law courts should impose the same penalty as if they were not addicts, emphasising that the punishment is a consequence of the anti-social action. In this way, the courts can help the addict to recover by not excusing anti-social action. We have thus argued that the sick role exists, but there are times when it should not be applied to specific illnesses!

Returning to the review of the different psychiatric illnesses, the dementias have become of increasing importance over the last fifty years, as they are often disorders of older people. In an ageing society, their prevalence is increasing and the pressure on society for resources to treat people with this very demanding condition are intense. Current knowledge means that a doctor with the requisite expertise can ensure that optimal use of valuable, recently developed medications goes alongside practical steps to minimise the effects of this disorder. Specialists in old age psychiatry have developed the greatest expertise in managing these conditions.

Schizophrenia and the affective disorders (hypomania and depressive illness) are seen very differently nowadays than in the days of the madhouse. A wealth of research has shown that they are more subtle disorders of brain function than the dementias. Hypomania refers to a condition in which mood is elevated to an inappropriate extent for prolonged periods of time, sometimes accompanied by abnormal beliefs (grandiose delusions), insomnia and spending of large amounts of money. In depressive psychosis, along with low mood and other physical changes such as loss of appetite, abnormal beliefs of guilt or worthlessness may be present, voices (of people not there) may be heard, and serious suicidal behaviour may occur.

In schizophrenia, patients may suffer the hearing of voices, sometimes talking about them; disturbances of thought (their confusion, or the loss of privacy of thought); and the development of bizarre beliefs. Although there are no cures for these illnesses, current treatment, based on both pharmacology and community supports, means that whereas such patients might have previously spent their lives in hospital, many can lead lives in the community, retaining their connections with those closest to them. Specialists in general adult psychiatry can provide treatment for both the acute phases of the disorder and for the longer term.

The neurotic disorders (as a classification) are a heterogeneous group. They include a number of conditions, such as obsessive-compulsive disorder, where there is increasing understanding that this is also (as with schizophrenia) a disorder for which there are changes in the brain that correspond with the clinical condition. Other disorders show another manifestation of the brain — that it is an organ supremely equipped to respond to the external environment. Awareness of the way the rest of the nervous system responds to external events is easily understood — few people would be impressed by the comment that if you put your hand near a fire, a series of nervous impulses along nerves in your arm, relayed in the spinal column will cause you to remove your hand, as a reflex.

But the brain co-ordinates response not just to the physical world, but also to the social world. Human beings behave as social animals. Social psychological brain functions such as provision of care and eliciting of care, unhappiness, shame, guilt, fear, anger, conscious and unconscious thoughts, are real phenomena — even if harder to quantify and demonstrate than, say, the number of bones in the hand, or the fracture of the shaft of a long bone. As with other complex mental functions, the brain changes that accompany these functions remain to be adequately demonstrated, but the neurotic disorders occur when such functions fail. Social disapproval may be handled by the brain by avoiding it, in a hysterical condition. Patients may experience fear in situations that are quite unthreatening, such as on seeing a harmless spider (phobia). Adverse social situations will properly elicit a moderate depressed mood, which itself becomes a problem when it is prolonged.

These psychological functions must have some purpose to be there in the first place. Anxiety indicates to the animal that there is a serious imminent danger and it must be prepared to respond. Depressed mood indicates that something is wrong in the psychosocial environment, and that steps must be taken to correct this. For example, depressed mood indicates to a person who has failed an exam that further steps need to be taken if this challenge is to be overcome in the longer term.

But not everyone feels able to respond to all the demands on them, from family, friends, work, and society in general. They exhibit their difficulties by showing signs of distress to those around them. Often the communications are clear; sometimes, they may take other forms. Some people may respond by focusing on the fatigue that accompanies trying to stay awake to meet demands of others; some may find that their bowel function is affected, with feelings of bloating or constipation; others may find that their sexual function is impaired. Patients may experience any of a large number of different physical symptoms, related to the response to demands made on them ('stress'). They may present to non-psychological doctors, who may investigate them for the possibility of a physical disorder without finding one. The symptoms may then be dismissed, followed by anger in the patient and frustration in the physician. But a careful assessment may reveal the presence of psychological factors that may be precipitating the physical symptoms. It should be remembered that a symptom is the experience of the patient and is always valid. Just because a physician cannot find one of a range of illnesses in his or her field of expertise does not mean that the patient does not experience what he or she claims to experience.

The diagnosis is important, as it will affect what treatment might be likely to be effective. And it should also be remembered at this stage that psychiatric diagnoses, such as irritable bowel syndrome, are not diagnoses of exclusion (ie. 'I can't think of a physical illness, so it must be all in the mind'), but real disorders in which the doctor must elicit the psychological factors that are causing the symptoms.

The patient may have some difficulty accepting that there is no life-threatening medical condition and may continue to perceive the doctor as the person to whom distress should be displayed. This is the process of hypochondriasis (where the patient has numerous medical symptoms and does not accept that there is no underlying illness, however much reassurance is offered) or Munchhausen's syndrome (in which the patient subconsciously feigns an illness). In both, the focus is on the process of obtaining caring behaviour from a health professional, rather than on any illness itself (though, confusingly, the patient will always refer to intractable physical symptoms). Usually, the health professional who is approached cannot respond adequately, sometimes followed by the doctor referring to the patient in a derogatory way (a 'heartsink' patient), rather than ensuring that the patient is transferred to the care of someone who can address the patient's distress.

For some patients, it is their response to the distress that becomes the concern of the doctor. They may respond by eating abnormally (the eating disorders, including anorexia nervosa) or by using psychoactive substances (the addictions), by deliberate self-harm (cutting oneself in non-dangerous areas) or by suicide attempts. If the patient constantly uses a set of behaviours to elicit such care, they may be seen as having a disorder of underlying personality.

The field of psychiatry, then, covers a wide spectrum: the complex brain diseases where behaviour alters dramatically and the entire spectrum of human responses to adversity. If you want to know about human life in its entirety, from the physical to the mental, you could do little better than to train as a medical practitioner and then specialise in psychiatry.

Am I suited to a career in psychiatry?

From the brief overview above, you may have gained some idea about whether or not psychiatry interests you. If it does, then you may want to explore it further. What can you do? Things that come immediately to mind would be to go to your local library and see if they have any books on psychology and psychiatry. Or you could look on the internet, especially at the website of the Royal College of Psychiatrists of the UK (www.rcpsych.ac.uk).

You may wish to ask your family and friends if they know anyone who has any connection with mental health. They may know a psychiatrist, a community psychiatric nurse or a psychiatric social worker. By speaking to them, you will get a sense of what it is like to work in mental health. You will get the day-to-day feeling, rather than just a dry sense of what the textbooks tell you. Your family may know someone who has been mentally ill and is willing to speak to you about their illness and their experiences of the treatment they received. Or you may wish to contact mental health self-help groups, such as MIND, who will tell you their version of what psychiatrists do. Do not feel you have to limit yourself to one person – talk to as many people as are willing to talk to you, and as you have time for.

It also helps to have a look at yourself. Think about what you have done in your life so far. Have you helped a friend out when he or she had a personal difficulty? Do you generally tend to find yourself listening to people when they talk about their personal problems? Have you done any work with disadvantaged groups, in either a voluntary or a paid capacity?

Or do you, perhaps, have an interest in brain research? Have you some particular interest in neurology, pharmacology, or psychology? What books do you tend to read? Do you like reading novels with a strong human touch? Or do you prefer to read more practical books? From these questions, you may gain an initial idea if psychiatry would suit you.

You may, of course, choose to try it out by applying for a junior job in psychiatry. You could take a substantive post, either on its own or on a rotation, or you may choose to take a job in a locum capacity. Allow yourself to remember that you always have the right to change your mind and that, if it does not go as you had hoped, you can always do something else. The experience gained in psychiatry will still serve you well in whatever else you do.

One particularly useful thing you can do is to see if you can meet some senior psychiatrists. If you are working as a junior doctor, you will either have a chance to work for one or, if you are working in another medical discipline, you will be able to contact local psychiatrists to ask for an informal meeting. While it is useful to talk to your peers and other young psychiatric trainees (especially about how things are in training rotations now), there is a particular benefit to be gained from talking informally to consultant-level doctors. That is because someone who has reached a consultant job – especially if they have been in it for some time – will be someone who is comfortable with the type of psychiatry they are doing. When you go to see a consultant (and assuming that he or she behaves in a pleasant manner towards you and is generally favourable to their branch of psychiatry) you will gain two things. The first is the actual information that they tell you. The second is whether you have a sense of liking or being similar to that person. This is important because, if you see similarities between yourself and the consultant, it may indicate that you would be happy doing the same job. Remember that if you complete training and reach the status of consultant or associate specialist, you will be doing that senior job for many more years than you will be doing professional training. It is not an infallible test, but if you can meet several people from different disciplines – and especially if you can meet someone who is a lovely person, but one you feel very different from – then you can compare better whether the consultant you think is similar to you actually is. When I was at an early stage of my postgraduate training, I met a charming surgeon and had a conversation with him. At the end of the meeting, I realised that, however well I regarded him, he and I were different animals. It was not the only reason that I chose not to be a surgeon, but it was a very helpful guide.

What am I letting myself in for?

If you decide that you do wish to proceed to a full psychiatric training, with the aim of becoming a consultant psychiatrist, the steps are as follows:

⌘ Obtain a place on an SHO general professional training scheme in psychiatry (usually lasting about three and a half years).
⌘ Pass the examination for the membership of the Royal College of Psychiatrists.
⌘ Obtain a place on a higher training scheme in psychiatry as a specialist registrar (another three to four years).
⌘ Gain your Certificate of Completion of Specialist Training and get your name included in the Specialist Register of the General Medical Council.
⌘ Obtain a consultant post.

This outline does not give a flavour of the diversity of the options available to you. There are a number of specialties and subspecialties. We have mentioned general adult psychiatry and old age psychiatry. Other main specialties are forensic psychiatry, child and adolescent psychiatry and learning disabilities. Subspecialties include neuropsychiatry, liaison psychiatry, addiction psychiatry, eating disorders, psychotherapy, puerperal psychiatry, psychopharmacology and an academic career.

You should not ignore the fact — which will be repeated throughout this book — that in the end, we all work to live, not live to work. It will be a minimum of seven years from start to finish, and may be more. You may choose to do all your training in one geographical area, you may not. As a qualified doctor, you will at the very least be in your mid-twenties and may be older. Who are the people coming on the ride with you, by default? Can your partner (and possibly children) live with what you are planning? What about your parents? Are these important considerations for you?

I am not suggesting that these are obstacles that cannot be overcome. The aim of this book is to help you deal with them, so that you can achieve your goal. I mention them because forewarned is forearmed.

Becoming a consultant psychiatrist (in my subspecialty of addiction) is one of the best things that ever happened to me. If you think it might be for you, read on.

2

Getting a training

You've decided that you would like to become a psychiatrist. But, where do you start? 'You look in the job advertisements in the medical press,' you reply. There are job advertisements in the *British Medical Journal* and *Hospital Doctor*, and you look under 'psychiatry'. That is the correct approach, but even with an advertisement, you need to know what you are looking for.

General professional training

If you want to train in the United Kingdom to be a psychiatrist, you need to get a medical qualification recognised by the General Medical Council and be fully registered (ie. you have done your house year). Only then can you apply for a general professional training in psychiatry. This means that you will need to work in several jobs as a senior house officer in psychiatry, in posts approved as suitable by the Royal College of Psychiatrists of the United Kingdom. Training posts usually last six months (occasionally they last nine months or one year). You can apply for one job at a time, but that is very demanding and unsettling. As a result, many medical schools have collected a number of posts to form a rotation. If you join a rotation, you will usually get a contract for three and a half or four years. You will then rotate through a series of posts without having to apply from scratch for each of them.

To get the best out of any training, you need to know what you need to know. The Royal College of Psychiatrists have posted the steps you need to take for training on their website (www.rcpsych.ac.uk). They have also posted a detailed curriculum that you can download. (You can ask the college to send you hard copies of these documents.) The documents of the college are necessarily rather brief. You need to have a better overview than the bare essentials of the formal regulations.

In short, to get a good grounding in psychiatry, you need to:

⌘ Get clinical experience.
⌘ Understand how new knowledge is obtained by research.

⌘ Understand how the quality of service delivery can be monitored (clinical audit).

⌘ Obtain a theoretical knowledge base and demonstrate that you have reached a satisfactory standard by passing the examination for the membership of the Royal College of Psychiatrists (the 'MRCPsych').

The clinical experience that you need to obtain involves seeing patients who have the conditions that psychiatrists treat and seeing examples of the different types of treatment that can be offered. You will need to see patients when they have acute crises and when their conditions are more settled and need a more measured, long-term consideration.

We introduced ourselves to the scope of psychiatry in *Chapter 1*. From the point of view of ensuring a comprehensive training, the spectrum of psychiatric conditions can usefully be considered by dividing them into three age groupings: child psychiatry; general adult psychiatry; and old age psychiatry.

Child psychiatry covers a range of conditions that arise from birth to late teens (different services have different cut-offs, often around sixteen or eighteen years). It includes the genetic and neurodevelopmental disorders, such as autism and Down's syndrome; disorders of social integration, such as conduct disorder and enuresis/encopresis; and childhood variants of adult psychiatric disorder, such as childhood schizophrenia or childhood depressive illness. In the case of the neurodevelopmental disorders, the early years are often managed by paediatricians. Psychiatrists take over when the children reach early adulthood (psychiatry of learning disability).

General adult psychiatry covers what many people think of as the bread and butter of psychiatry: schizophrenia and manic-depressive disorder, neurotic depression and the anxiety disorders. There are a number of other conditions, such as hysteria, obsessive-compulsive disorder and personality disorder. General adult psychiatrists may also have to manage patients with disorders for which subspecialists can be found, such as the addictions (alcohol, illicit drugs); the eating disorders (anorexia nervosa, bulimia nervosa and morbid obesity); and the psychosomatic conditions (eg. irritable bowel syndrome, fibromyalgia).

Old age psychiatry covers conditions that are more common after the age of sixty-five, such as the dementias (Alzheimer's disease, multi-infarct dementia, Parkinsonian dementia, etc); depression in the elderly; and schizophrenia in the elderly.

Of course, these distinctions are artificial and there are areas of overlap. For example, should a thirty-eight-year-old man who has a dementing condition as a result of a road-traffic accident be managed by a general adult psychiatrist or an old age psychiatrist? These are serious practical issues for the different services in the case of patients whose conditions do not fit neatly into the age division into child, adult and old age psychiatry.

From a training perspective, the three types of psychiatrist cover broadly different types of condition. The implication is that in a properly constructed training portfolio, a trainee should be exposed to each of these groups of psychiatric condition. Moreover, different conditions require different treatment. The major advance in the twentieth century in respect of the management of schizophrenia was the discovery that a group of pharmacological agents, the neuroleptics, are effective in alleviating the symptoms. It is not a placebo effect; it is not a non-specific effect. Neuroleptics treat psychosis; benzodiazepines, β-blockers, steroids, *Mars* bars do not. If you want to be a psychiatrist, you have to learn about psychopharmacology (apart from reading the chapter on drugs acting on the central nervous system in the *British National Formulary*, you could look at Cookson [2002] for a detailed but useful overview).

Children, usually, grow up in families. Often, if a child is showing signs of distress — enough for the child to be referred to a child psychiatrist — it is almost certainly because of something going on in the family. Treatment of the child will involve looking at the family, seeing what might be going on, and trying to alleviate any difficulties. The process is formally known as family therapy and it is an example of a psychotherapy. There are many different types of psychotherapy and you need to know about them. Brown, Pedder and Bateman (2000) provide an excellent overview.

Currently, it is a requirement that each candidate for the MRCPsych has some clinical experience of psychotherapy, and you would be required to take on one case (under specialist supervision) for cognitive-behavioural therapy and one for individual psychotherapy with a psychodynamic component. We also have to consider the context of treatment — considerably more than in other branches of medicine.

People with mental illnesses may commit a number of acts that are against the law. It may be that they are doing so rationally — a person with a mental illness who sees a car door open, with the keys in the ignition, may make the decision to drive the car away. It is no different from someone who does not have a mental disorder.

But sometimes a person will commit an act as a result of mental disorder that they would not commit if they were well. For example, a person may assault another because of a delusionary belief that the other person was the Devil and that by assaulting him, the patient would reduce the amount of evil in the world. After treatment for the psychotic state, the patient may realise what he has done and regret it bitterly. The law wishes to acknowledge that some people break the law as a result of mental illness and wishes to take account of it in delivering punishments. Any psychiatrist can give evidence about a person's mental state, but the frequency with which the courts request psychiatric evidence has given rise to the subspecialty of forensic psychiatry. Along with experience in child psychiatry, adult psychiatry and old age psychiatry, a trainee should gain some experience in the forensic aspects of psychiatry.

Ever-growing medical knowledge and its rapid dissemination through information technology, particularly the internet, means that it is possible to provide a constantly improving standard of care for patients. The practitioner must keep abreast of developments in his or her field. Psychiatric trainees can gain some experience of research by incorporating a research post into their portfolio of jobs, or they may undertake a piece of research (under supervision) in their spare time. Occasionally, they may be given the time and fees to undertake a higher degree, such as an MSc. The most simple mechanism of doing research is to attend a journal club, where a trainee can understand how research is done. In this way, the trainee can learn how to evaluate papers subsequently published in the medical press to see how well the authors' claims stand up to scrutiny.

For those trainees who are interested in the possibility of a career in academic psychiatry, a conflict arises. Academics will encourage a fledgling academic to undertake research at the earliest stage, as greater experience and competence is gained in this way. However, it is this author's view that you cannot research a condition that you do not understand, and that the basis of all medicine is extensive clinical experience and expertise. Trainees who have not reached the level of the MRCPsych do not have the clinical experience to undertake meaningful research.

Higher psychiatric training

In the UK, once you have undertaken a general professional training for about three and a half years and obtained the MRCPsych, you are not regarded as fully trained. Currently, you are required to undertake a further period of training, referred to as higher training. At the end of this, you can receive a Certificate of Completion of Specialist Training and your name can appear on the Specialist Register of the General Medical Council under the specialty of psychiatry.

On a practical level, there are those who might decide at this stage to cease training to pursue another path. Options include setting up in private practice (although it is possible that they may not be recognised by medical insurance companies for the purpose of benefit) and taking a job with the pharmaceutical industry. Some decide that they do not wish to take a consultant post and wish to work as a staff grade doctor or associate specialist. But many, if not most, of those who pass the MRCPsych and work in the UK will wish to proceed to train to become a consultant.

In the period of higher training, the position filled by the trainee is referred to as a specialist registrar (SpR). Current arrangements require that each trainee has his or her own national training number (NTN). The number of NTNs is limited. The purpose of this period of higher training is to allow the trainee the opportunity to increase his or her clinical experience and to intensify the depth of knowledge of the proposed consultant position. It is an oft-repeated maxim in medical training that 'common things are common'. This applies to clinical situations as well as clinical conditions. As a fully trained practitioner, the specialist has to refer to his or her own repertoire of clinical experiences to decide what to do in any given new clinical situation. For example, a psychiatrist may be asked to assess a patient in a new type of specialist prison. If the psychiatrist has visited many prisons before, he or she will have a basic understanding of how to approach the prison system and can apply this to the new situation.

The specialist registrar grade is also an opportunity to try things out. Because the core clinical work takes up only three of the work days, the SpR has the opportunity to experience other clinical opportunities (taking on a psychotherapy patient if he/she has not already done so as an SHO, for example, or seeing some patients in a specialty not already tried).

In some respects, the SpR is a trainee consultant. Apart from acting up for the consultant during periods of the consultant's absence, the SpR can learn some of the non-clinical tasks that consultants are asked to perform. The SpR can gain experience of teaching doctors in junior grades, training for examinations and even organising professional examinations. The SpR can carry out an audit of clinical practice. The SpR can gain some insight into the way that management processes occur in a complex organisation such as the NHS by sitting in on the various managerial committees (eg. the local medical advisory committee, the committee by which the consultants decide on the advice they will give the trust board and where matters of common interests to the consultants can be discussed) that are essential to the running of the hospital or the trust.

By this time, the SpR will have enough basic knowledge of psychiatry to be able to participate usefully in a research project. SpRs who are training as clinicians will only have one day a week for a research project, which is usually insufficient. Lecturers (honorary SpRs) will have more time for research, but less time for widening the clinical expertise.

The SpR needs to see the period of higher training (usually organised through a higher training scheme of a medical school) as an opportunity to gain depth of clinical experience and width of knowledge. Although the SpR may be offered a total of four one-year postings, it is useful to see the period as a whole, as some aspects are better carried out in one posting than in another.

Part-time training

The recognition over recent years that doctors have a life outside medicine has led to the development of schemes in which doctors can work less than full time, both in a substantive capacity and as trainees. While the most obvious circumstance for a person to request part-time training is that of a parent (usually a mother) bringing up small children, there are a host of reasons why a person may not wish to work full time.

While it is, admittedly, more convenient for the employing organisation to employ one full-time person than two part-time staff, it is important that people wishing to work part-time should feel able to assert their request. As with all matters of dispute, it is a matter of both sides working in a spirit of mutual co-operation that will achieve the result that is acceptable to all concerned. What is important is to realise that, if you have a reason for working part time, you should not feel brow-beaten by some hospital employee into feeling that you have to put your needs secondary to the needs of the hospital (which may have difficulties arising from your decision to work part time — but that is not your problem). You will, of course, have to convince someone why you wish to train part time, but if we are talking about part-time training, once you have convinced the interview panel that you are suitable for appointment to a general or a higher training rotation, you have the right to assert your request to work part time rather than full time. It is up to you to present your reasons and stand by them.

Having been accepted as a part-time trainee, you will have to fulfil the requirements in place at the time. For example, if you work five sessions per week, then it may be that you are asked to work for seven years at this rate to be regarded as having (from a training perspective) three and a half years of work at ten sessions per week.

If you take this on, you do not have to feel like a second-class citizen; you are simply another employee with a different contract. Nor should you feel that you have to prove yourself by working more than your contracted hours. If the service has agreed with you that you will work five sessions per week, then you should go home after you have done them. You do not have to take additional work home just so you can give the impression that you are not 'letting the side down'. Once you have been appointed, you should work with your consultant trainer (and manager, if a different person) to develop a timetable in which your entire workload (clinical and training) can be fitted into the time contracted. If that leaves the service with tasks that are not being done, it is the responsibility of the manager and the consultant to make alternative arrangements — not yours.

There is now a moderate body of literature about working as a part-time doctor in the NHS (see *Chapter 6*) and you should consult it.

Selecting a rotation

Only you can decide what sort of life you want. And you should include it in your decision about which rotation you are prepared to join. What is not appropriate is to apply to a rotation because you are given some notion that it is somehow 'the best'. The best rotation for you is the one that is right for you, and the one that is right for you is the one that fits best with your goals, needs and aspirations. This is not just a matter of 'being nice'. If you are put under undue pressure on a rotation, or face demands that you cannot meet, you will not be happy. Workers who are happy produce better work than those who are not.

If you are of an age to marry and have children, there are other considerations. Being a parent – even as a psychiatrist – is an immense demand. (I will return to this theme later in more detail.) At this stage, what is important is that you think very carefully about your social network – in particular, your access to parents and siblings, who might be willing to help out in all sorts of ways; your access to friends who may lighten or share the burden; and your access to good schools. These are all matters that you should include in your decision about where to apply. If you have a good relationship with your parents who live, say, in Bristol, and you live in Bath, you may want to think very carefully before applying to a rotation in the north of England. And vice versa for someone, say, in Newcastle.

For all doctors, other aspects of personal life should not be disregarded. You should think carefully before leaving the community of your church, mosque or synagogue. You should question whether you want to work on a rotation in a geographical area where, for example, homophobia is common if you are gay; or if horseriding or surf-boarding or supporting Arsenal are important to you, you should not feel you have to give up these things to get a training. Before you enquire about any rotation that you see advertised, ask yourself if you would be prepared to live there. What might you gain by moving (if you had to) — and what might you lose?

If you do decide to respond to an advertisement for a rotation, you will be sent an information pack. Most packs start with a description of the location and its facilities. Look also at the geographical circumstances of the jobs on the rotation. Although many jobs will be concentrated around the teaching hospitals, a few may be some distance from the centre. Would you have to work at one of these hospitals? If so, would it bother you? And if it was highly inconvenient, how would the rotation deal with your request not to be placed there?

Having decided that a given rotation is in a geographical area acceptable to you, and having obtained the information pack, you need to check that it will provide the right training for your purposes.

For an SHO training scheme, you need to note how many jobs there are and what proportion of specialties. Will you be able to obtain a comprehensive training? Will you be able to get exposure to all three of the basic groups (child psychiatry, adult psychiatry and old age psychiatry) and some forensic experience? In the days of my own SHO rotation, there were (I think) twenty-four posts. Only two of them were for child psychiatry, and each of those posts was for one year. Given that we spent an average of four years on the rotation, each trainee had only a one-in-three chance of a child psychiatry placement.

Similarly, when considering an SpR rotation, look at the distribution of the jobs. You will have already chosen a subspecialty by applying to a general adult SpR rotation or a child psychiatry or old age psychiatry or forensic psychiatry or psychotherapy rotation, but will you get the breadth and depth that you need?

Look also at the support you would get. Does the rotation have adequate libraries? Is there sufficient access to the internet and can you get information from there? Are there regular meetings of SHOs and SpRs. Are there case conferences, journal clubs and academic lectures? Do the trainees get on with the trainers, individually and collectively?

Some of these questions you can answer from the literature that you are sent by the medical personnel staff. Other questions can be answered by contacting doctors already working on the rotation. Some may be too busy, but others may be willing to talk to you. Make sure that you speak to more than one person to get a balanced and rounded view of the rotation.

Other questions are best answered when you visit. All organisations will, rightly, present themselves in the best light possible. We live in an age when euphemisms are rife (when an estate agent, for example, tells you that the place is quaint and adaptable to your requirements, you find a small dingy flat in need of a lot of repair). When you visit, you might get a sense of the place from the state of the buildings. Speak to as many members of staff as you can — not just doctors, but everyone who will talk to you. The secretary, the receptionist, the porter will all have views on how the place is working; you will gain a sense if people are happy working there or not.

Also, talk to any consultants and managers who will meet with you. When you go for an 'informal' visit, you should be aware that, despite the word 'informal', you are being weighed up by everyone you meet. But the consultant and manager are also on trial with you. If a consultant says that he or she has been there for twenty years and plans to stay on until retirement, and you pick up that you are not going to get along with that person, you may want to think twice about working there.

In the case of a rotation, it is not possible to visit every hospital or speak to every consultant and manager. But you can get a sense of the overall rotation from one or two selected visits. The current trainees may be able to guide you.

The same approach is useful for both SHO and SpR rotations. However, if you have done an SHO rotation in one place, you may wish to think about doing your SpR rotation elsewhere (if feasible). If you do this, you will widen your clinical experience and see different ways of doing things. You will have the opportunity to avoid the rut of 'this is how we have always done it' and be able to reflect more on your clinical practice.

Applying for a job

Application form and *curriculum vitae* (CV)

The formal process of applying for a job seems daunting at first, but it is much more straightforward than it seems. If a hospital has three posts for an SHO in psychiatry, what it wants are three people who are suitable and willing to do the job.

The process of job selection is not an exam. There is no pass or fail. The jobs are offered to suitable candidates and you either get one or you do not. If there are 300 equally qualified applicants for three jobs, then you are in a crowd of 297 if you are not one of the successful applicants. If there are only two applicants for the three jobs, then, unless you are entirely unsuitable (eg. you are not medically qualified), you are likely to be offered a job.

If you decide to apply for a job, you will be asked to fill in an application form and often (but not always) to include a *curriculum vitae* (CV). The information pack sent by the hospital or medical school should contain, as well as the blank application form for you to fill in, a person specification. This should list the essential and desirable attributes for a person doing the job. For example, for an SHO post, it may be specified that a medical practitioner is required. If you do not have a medical degree (or if your degree is not yet recognised by the UK's General Medical Council), there is no point in applying. If there is a desirable quality, eg. previous experience working with the mentally ill, you should not worry if you do not meet the criteria. However, you should be aware that you may be asked in the interview about whether you have some alternative experience that would bring some additional positive quality to the job. If the desirable quality is that you have previously held an SHO post in psychiatry, do not worry if you have not done so. However, if you did an elective in psychiatry as a medical student, you should not omit to mention it at this stage.

The application form is often a standard form. It may be very general, for use with all staff — not just doctors. Bear in mind that you may have to fill it in by hand. Irrespective of the information in the text, the neatness of your writing and the legibility and ordering of the text on the page will be the first truly personal information you give about yourself. It does not look good if this is shoddy, even if the content reveals a genius. Take time and fill in the form carefully and neatly.

There may be a space for you to write why you are applying for this job. Put the reasons down as neatly and as enthusiastically as you can. But do not try to convey enthusiasm if you do not feel it. It is often easy to gain the impression that someone is trying too hard to convince the reader. If the person receiving the application form is not convinced that the person wants the job, he or she may wonder whether the applicant has given the job sufficient thought.

Unlike the application form, the CV is your opportunity to tell your potential employer what you want them to know. Again, presentation is important. Few potential employers would be impressed by a handwritten CV: they would expect candidates for a medical position to have access to a word processor. If you do not have access to a word processor, you should state why not clearly.

In selecting the information to include, ask yourself what is relevant for the post you are applying for. The organisation that is seeking an employee will want to know:

- your basic details and how to contact you
- your previous education and occupational history, in as much detail as is relevant for the post
- information about you as a person, such as your interests
- two or three professional referees (as requested).

Your basic details should include your name, professional address and contact telephone number. Some will add their age, sex, marital status and number of children. You should clarify which name is your surname, and your title (eg. Mr, Mrs, Ms, etc). You should only include a nickname if it is how you are known to others (eg. a previous consultant who has agreed to act as a referee). Your school history should be brief and just a summary. Your occupational history should be a complete record (though brief where appropriate). For example, after completing a training as a physician and obtaining the MRCP, if you were applying for an SpR post in cardiology, you would list all the jobs; the names of the consultants; what you did in each job; and what medical procedures you are proficient in. But if you were changing career direction and applying for a training in psychiatry, it would be sufficient to record that you had been on the 'X' hospital school of medicine rotation in general medicine for 'Y' years, and had obtained the MRCP. Conversely, if applying for a higher training in psychiatry, you should include details of your experience in SHO posts.

Do not worry if your CV is short, if this is appropriate. If you are applying for an SHO rotation after completing your house jobs, the occupational history will necessarily be brief. Do not include unnecessary padding. For higher training, you should include any experience that you have had in non-medical areas of your work, such as teaching, audit and research, and managerial-type activities (eg. junior doctors' representative). There should be no gaps in your occupational history: if you have had time out of medicine, then you should include it and say why.

As your personal information, you should include your interests and hobbies. As with previous parts of the CV, do not include padding. It will be clear to any interview panel that a busy junior doctor has not got time to pursue twenty different activities and hobbies.

Bear in mind that you can be asked at interview about anything that you write on an application form or CV. This is particularly important when it comes to the personal-information section. If you put down that you are interested in the theatre, you cannot complain if you are asked if this interest has somehow led you into considering a career in psychiatry. (The answer may be 'no', but that does not make the question unfair.)

Finally, you should include the names and professional addresses of people who are willing to provide a reference for you. The application form will specify how many references are required. Your current employer will almost certainly be required.

You should always ask a person before putting his or her name down as a referee. This is not just a matter of courtesy, but has certain practical implications. It is not unknown for a prospective employer to telephone a referee. If you have not asked, your consultant may be somewhat surprised by the call — putting you in a bad light. Also, consultants are busy people. Requests for references can come at short notice. It is much easier for a consultant to respond in time if he or she is aware that such a request may be made. (Of course, there is some concern about references, based on a misunderstanding of what a reference is, and its legal status. As I am not a lawyer, I cannot discuss this in any depth. It would be better to explore the issue, if necessary, with somebody who has a legal training.)

Employers are required to provide references if asked. They do not have the right to refuse. If a consultant says to you, 'If you don't do this, I won't give you a reference,' he or she is on shaky ground. You may be able to take legal action for this; or for anything else that is written about you, if defamatory. However, a future employer may also be able to take legal action if your consultant omits anything material (eg. if your consultant fails to pass on to a child psychiatrist who plans to employ you that you were subject to an allegation of improper conduct with younger patients).

A reference must be fair, accurate and reasonable. A wise referee will write something that is as objective as possible. The structure that I have used myself is as follows:

⌘ Re: Dr Joe Bloggs.

⌘ Thank you for asking for a reference about Dr Bloggs for the post of SpR in psychiatry.

⌘ Details of Dr Bloggs working with me.
   ❖ (Dr Bloggs was the SHO on my firm in the Addiction Unit at St Wherever's Hospital between August 1927 and January 1928.)

⌘ Details of his work on the ward/team.
   ❖ (Dr Bloggs managed a caseload of twenty patients in a competent manner.)

⌘ Details of his educational progress (in a training post).
   ❖ (While he was on the firm, he passed the MRCPsych.)

⌘ Details of relations with work colleagues.
   ❖ (He was well-liked by other medical and nursing staff on the firm during his time with us.)

⌘ Opinion about suitability for the post
   ❖ (He is well-suited for the position of SpR in psychiatry).

I have made it a practice to agree a draft reference with an SHO before sending it out.

The London Deanery is currently using structured reference forms and advising referees that they show the reference to applicants on request. When you send in your application, you should keep a copy of your CV and application form. It is advisable to keep these copies beyond this application, because you may apply for further posts some time in the future and, even when no deception is intended, it is easy to write different things on different forms at different times. Even if no charges are made, it still leaves you with a lot of explaining to do.

Interviews

The interview is only the final stage of the selection process. Evaluation has started with the informal visits, the application form and the CV. It is a formal process. Your presentation of yourself is as important as the answers you give to the questions. You should dress appropriately, as this can be part of convincing the interview panel that you are ready to step into the job. If you are applying to be an SHO or SpR in psychiatry, you should dress as one.

Plan carefully to make sure that you arrive in good time for the interview. Be sure about the time of the interview, where the interview is, accurate directions for getting there, and the transport details all well in advance. If in doubt, contact the personnel officer who is making the arrangements. If you are delayed on your way to the interview for reasons beyond your control, make sure that you have a contact number for the administrator on the day.

If you are invited for interview, you should recognise that it remains the purpose of the process to assess your suitability for the job. The interview panel should be appropriate. You may ask the personnel officer for the names and posts of the people on the panel, if these details are not already supplied in advance.

It is increasingly recognised that candidates should be assessed on objective criteria as far as possible, identified in the personal specification. As a result, you should be able to anticipate the majority of the questions.

For an SHO post you may be asked: why you want to do psychiatry; your previous medical experience; any previous additional education (eg. a BSc in neurology, psychiatry or pharmacology); any research you may have done; and anything you have done in your private life that is relevant to psychiatry. You may also be asked a question designed to make you 'think on your feet', but related to the subject. For example, if there has been a recent story on the news of a crime committed by a patient with schizophrenia, you may be asked what you think should be done with him or her. You should read the newspapers and listen to the news on TV or radio in the days before the interview for any story that might be of interest to a psychiatrist and might lead to a question at your interview. If you anticipate correctly, you can plan some replies.

For an SpR post, you may be asked about: your experience as an SHO; your reasons for choosing the sub-branch of psychiatry for which you are being interviewed; any audit or research you have undertaken; and any experience you have of teaching or of managerial issues. Again, you may be asked a question that requires you to 'think on your feet', but this may just as easily come from the medical press (eg. *British Medical Journal, The Lancet, British Journal of Psychiatry*) or from a recent political position document (any proposed change to the Mental Health Act, for example). The answers here are not those of the MRCPsych exam: they will test whether you can keep up-to-date with clinical developments and form an independent clinical opinion. After all, this is what you will have to do as a consultant.

With all the questions you are asked, there is no right or wrong answer. Your answers will indicate whether you have the experience and potential to undertake the training at a given time. You should not try to 'second guess' the person asking the question.

You should also consider that you have a right to expect reasonable questions that do not contain any discriminatory material. If you are a woman, for example, you cannot be asked at interview if you are going to leave the rotation to have children. For either sex, your sexual orientation or religious beliefs are irrelevant. The only issue is whether you are likely to be able to do the job adequately. You also have the protection of knowing that you have the right to request to see all comments written down by the panel during the course of the interview.

Naturally, you will feel some anxiety when you come to the interview. You should be treated courteously. When you are asked questions, you may find that you respond more slowly than normal because of your anxiety. The interview panel will understand this. If there is any question that you do not understand, ask for it to be repeated or asked in another way. This is entirely acceptable.

When the panel has asked all their questions, you will be asked if you have any questions. You should treat this question as a formality, and the answer should be 'no', as you should have visited and spoken to people and found out the answers to any concerns you might have before the interview. This is not the time to discuss salary, what the job entails, or any specific requests you may have, should you be appointed. The panel does not have the authority to solve any problems on behalf of the organisation. After the interview, you will either be asked to wait or for a contact telephone number.

If you are offered a post, you should acknowledge the offer, awaiting the confirmation in writing. It is when you receive the letter offering you the job that you can contact the personnel officer to deal with any specific enquiries. At that stage, you can clarify such issues as the salary.

Getting a contract

Once you have been appointed to a post and accepted the offer, a contract exists. (If you specifically need to know, a lawyer will tell you exactly when.) You do not have to have a written document for the contract to exist. However, it is always helpful to have something written, as it reduces the possibility of dispute afterwards.

In the NHS, there is a tendency to use relatively standard contracts, and you are unlikely to have conditions significantly different from your colleagues. Your contract should say certain standard things:

⌘ What your job is (this may need to be read in conjunction with the job description, which you should have received with your information pack prior to applying for the job). You should, ideally, have a clear statement of the actual tasks required ('duties of the post') rather than a vague notion ('the postholder will see outpatients' – how many patients? How many sessions?).

⌘ What you will be paid, including a statement of what amount of annual and study leave is included.

⌘ Issues relating to termination of the contract (by either side), discipline and dismissal.

⌘ A statement that the contract details (especially the nature of the postholder's medical duties) can only be changed by the mutual agreement of both sides.

There are also external rules that will affect the contract, such as the European Working Time Directive, which limits the amount of work that any person can do in one week. Nevertheless, it is useful to have a copy of the written contract and you should ask the personnel officer for it. Keep copies of all correspondence with the personnel officer after accepting the job and before you have a contract you are happy with.

It is important to realise that, in NHS medical postgraduate training posts, you are an employee. This means that you are only required to perform the duties specified in your contract. You do not have to do anything else. If you are asked to do any additional duties, you may choose to agree to do them; but you do not have to, however much pressure, appropriate or otherwise, managers put on you. (Make sure that you know how to deal with bullying managers and their demands [*Chapter 4*].) You should never forget that you have the right to decline additional duties. To illustrate this, consider a case reported in *The Times* (27 August, 2003): 'Consultants... [at one hospital]... had been issued with dusters and plastic rubbish sacks and asked to clean their offices themselves.' This was said to be because, 'The NHS Trust overspent its budget by £7 million last year and managers said the move was an important part of its recovery plan.' Whatever the truth of the report, it should be clear that doctors are employed to provide medical services, not cleaning services. The responsibility for the financial problems lies with the managers, not with the doctors. It is hoped that the doctors in question asserted that they were not employed to provide cleaning services and that the hospital had a duty to ensure that they could work in clean conditions.

The workings of a rotation

A rotation is a series of psychiatric jobs, linked together. There is usually a clinical tutor who takes responsibility for the allocation of jobs to individuals. Commonly, the doctors on a rotation are invited at each rotation point (the time when they change jobs) to apply for the next one. A good clinical tutor will attempt to ensure that all doctors have the opportunity to work in posts that meet their overall training needs. Thus, although a trainee may make a request for a particular post, this may on occasion have to be denied, either because too many people have applied for this post or because the trainee's portfolio will not look balanced with this post.

The clinical tutor will also probably want to ensure that 'political' considerations are included in the thinking. For example, on some rotations, the jobs at the teaching hospital are often seen as more desirable than those in the district general hospitals, as they give the opportunity for trainees to cultivate *protégé* relationships with academics who they think will assist their career to a greater degree. Or some jobs are seen as less demanding and therefore permit more time for study for the examination. The clinical tutor may wish to ensure that all trainees have roughly equal access to the jobs that are regarded as more desirable. After a trainee is denied a job they have requested on one occasion, it may be possible to request that it is offered at the next rotation point.

Getting the best out of each job

For many years, the training provided by doctors could at best be described as amateurish. Juniors would come into post and be expected to 'get on with it', whatever that might mean. Maxims such as, 'see one, do one, teach one' sounded good, but in reality it left highly inexperienced doctors thrashing about in the hope that they would somehow come out of it all right. Of course, doctors in postgraduate training are intelligent, educated people who are determined to do the best for their patients. As a result, doctors have learnt a great deal during the course of such unsupervised training. But, the results are patchy. Different doctors learnt different things to different degrees.

Training, even at postgraduate level, must involve the transmission of defined skills and competences. A curriculum gives an overview of the basic knowledge a psychiatrist might be expected to have; the training programme should be tailored to ensure that the trainee is directed to obtain the required clinical knowledge and is given the opportunity to acquire the requisite skills.

Each job on the rotation gives the trainee the opportunity to acquire two types of skill:

⌘ Generic skills that are basic to psychiatry and transferable between psychiatric disciplines. Empathic listening and knowledge of the principles of psychopharmacology are examples of such generic skills.
⌘ Specific skills that are relevant only to the individual discipline. Motivational interviewing, a technique designed to help addicted people decide to cease the harmful drug use, is an example of a specific skill.

The distinction between generic and specific skills is not hard and fast, but in reviewing progress over the whole of the rotation, it is possible to look at the range of generic skills and try to ensure that they are acquired over the course of the rotation. Gaps identified at the end of one job may be addressed in another.

It is important that the clinical tutor, along with his or her consultant colleague, should identify those skills and knowledge base. Having done so, each trainee should be given such a list with a view to ensuring that they obtain them over the course of the rotation. (Such clarity about training may not yet be available on all rotations.) This should then be applied to each training post. A trainee should be advised at the start of each posting what training goals might be achieved in the course of the attachment. These should be clear and composed of objective criteria. The trainee should then be constantly monitored through the clinical supervisory system to ensure that the objectives are being met. Finally, at the end of the attachment, the trainee should sit with the trainer to summarise what has been achieved in the course of the attachment, and what gaps might be addressed at a future stage of training. This can be achieved in a formal way if the trainee undergoes induction and goal-setting at the beginning of the job; weekly supervision with the use of trainee log books in the course of the job; and assessment and appraisal at the end of the job.

Induction

Doctors in training who are starting a new post may be visiting the hospital where they will be working for the first time. On the first day of the post, the organisers of a good psychiatric rotation will have arranged for an induction programme at which attendance by new doctors is compulsory. The organisers will have arranged for the consultant trainers to have released the junior doctor for the day.

The aim of induction should be to provide the new staff member with the most essential information needed to start carrying out the job. In the case of the rotational trainee doctor, he or she needs to know general details about the working of the hospital, as well as specific details about their own job. The initial induction for all trainees on a given psychiatric rotational scheme should include all the doctors. A crucial task is to make all new doctors feel welcome, and to assure them that the work they will do in the post is valuable.

In addition to the formal information imparted, the induction meeting will give the trainees the opportunity to meet one another informally and to get to know colleagues with whom they will be working. It will also set up the network by which a whole mass of informal information can be imparted between peers. Support by peers can occur in the course of the six-, nine- or twelve-month period before the next rotational point.

The formal information will vary, depending on local needs, but will probably include:

⌘ Information about the hospital:
  ❖ The structure of the building (a tour of the building may be organised); the staff and department on sites; how medical investigations are obtained, including the availability of phlebotomy services; where food may be obtained; parking and accommodation arrangements; fire drill and security services; other general facilities available (banks, newsagents, etc); occupational health arrangements; and medical personnel.
⌘ Information about the rotational arrangements:
  ❖ The rota; the on-call rooms; tasks that have to be shared generally; educational opportunities available on site (journal

clubs, case conferences, academic lectures, libraries and other sources of information, research opportunities, exam preparations); the availability of psychotherapy training.

⌘ Essential practical information about provision of psychiatric services:
   ❖ What services are available locally; expectations of local GPs; how to contact specialist services that are off site; how patients are admitted in an emergency; bed manager and how to obtain senior support (SpR for SHOs, consultant for SpRs) when on-call; any local formulary and local medical committee decisions about which medications may be prescribed by junior and senior staff; access to social services and, in particular, how to contact the duty approved social worker; emergency arrangements for a patient who meets the criteria for child psychiatry or old age psychiatry.

⌘ Essential psychiatric clinical information:
   ❖ Assessment of a patient; management of violence; management of manipulative behaviour.

⌘ Miscellaneous clinical:
   ❖ Cardiopulmonary resuscitation update training.

⌘ Administration:
   ❖ List and contact details of important people.

It should be remembered that an induction day is extremely tiring. Although the organiser will want to pack in as much information as possible, the day should finish early and the trainees should have the opportunity to relax in the evening. If possible, a trainee who has previously worked in that hospital should be asked to take the on-call for that day.

After you have been inducted generally into the hospital, you will need to have an induction into your new job. This should be carried out by the consultant trainer and not a deputy. A dedicated time should be made available for this, and interruptions should not be permitted except in the direst clinical emergency. Should it not be possible for the job induction to be completed at one sitting, it is crucial that adequate arrangements be made in the very near future for its completion.

The induction to the post should include a tour of the department — ward, outpatients (if on site) and any other facility, such as day hospital and/or occupational therapy department — and an introduction to key staff. You should ideally be handed a list of the names of all relevant staff, their location, job titles and contact details. The induction should also include an explanation by the consultant trainer of the job that you will be carrying out, and how it fits in with the work of the unit.

As well as introducing the job, the consultant trainer should give you some suggestions of what the training goals of the job should be. There will be specific learning goals related to the job (the specialist provision by this firm of one aspect of general psychiatric services – e.g. rehabilitation in schizophrenia; an introduction to a subspecialty, such as learning disability, eating disorder, liaison psychiatry or addiction). These goals should be impersonal and objective. For example, in any discipline, the full assessment of new patients is an instructive process for inexperienced trainees, especially if the case is thoroughly discussed with the consultant trainer. It is a straightforward goal for the consultant trainer to suggest that you should aim to see a given (realistic) number of new patients in the course of your attachment (allowing for the fact that there will be a number of new patients who will not attend their outpatient appointments).

Other similarly objective goals and aims should be agreed. The goals may well fall into several categories:

⌘ Acquiring a basic competence in the assessment and management of the patient group specific to the firm.
⌘ Acquiring a basic theoretical knowledge, or enhancing previous theoretical knowledge, of the clinical conditions treated on the firm.
⌘ Acquiring knowledge of topics relevant to administrative management, both in theory and occasionally in practice (for example, an SHO might seek to be a junior doctor representative; an SpR might undertake a small audit project or shadow a manager for a day).
⌘ Preparing for the MRCPsych examination (for SHOs) or teaching and organisation of the MRCPsych (for SpRs).
⌘ Joining or continuing a research project group.
⌘ Career development in its broadest sense.

Not all the categories may be relevant to a given trainee at different stages of his or her training.

It is crucial to realise that you have the right to question the goals suggested by your consultant trainer and to make your own suggestions. Ideally, your conversation with the trainer will review your previous experience and tailor the choice of goals to meet your training needs. The consultant trainer will, of course, wish to indicate the nature of the relationship he or she expects to have with you. The trainer should help you develop your timetable, including both the regular clinical meetings that you would be expected to attend, and the weekly slot when your trainer will meet with you for supervision. The meetings and commitments that you include in your timetable should be selected to assist you in meeting the agreed training goals.

In my view, your trainer should indicate that it is his or her role to support your work. He or she should indicate his or her availability to you at times of clinical difficulty and how you may contact the trainer urgently. It should be considered that your relationship with your trainer should be professional – you are a junior colleague, not a skivvy – and your trainer should treat you with the same courtesy that you should show him or her. A practical point is that boundaries should be respected. You work for a limited number of hours in the day. When the day is over, you should expect to go home. Even as a professional, you should not be expected to stay more than a few minutes at most (except in emergency clinical circumstances) beyond the end of your contracted hours. It is no longer appropriate for hospitals to expect their employed medical staff to work regularly several unpaid extra hours per day. Unless you give your express permission, your trainer should not contact you at home.

A good trainer will also recognise the importance of being adequately rested when you come to work. You should be invited to book the weeks of your leave entitlement. In a short posting, this can seem unduly hasty to raise early, but if you do not do so it may be some time before leave can be taken, leading possibly to it having to be taken at one time. This is disruptive for a firm, so if you and your trainer can incorporate discussion of leave arrangements from the beginning, proper intervals can be allowed between periods of leave and the firm can make proper arrangements to cover your absence. And, it means that you *can* go to your sister's wedding in Australia.

Not all trainers will agree with my view of the relationship between a consultant and junior colleague. You will need to get an early understanding of your consultant trainer's way of working.

The trainer should also indicate any issues specific to the job you are doing. For example, in my specialty of addiction, one of the clinical features is the frequent errors of communication. Addicted patients may at times interpret staff behaviour differently to the way that the staff intended. In some circumstances, a naive staff member may put him or herself in professional danger. Should a doctor perform a physical examination (especially if there is any examination of intimate parts of the body) on an addicted patient, the patient may interpret routine clinical practice as a sexual or physical assault — and a complaint may be made. The staff member would therefore be wise to perform a physical examination on an addicted patient only in the presence of a professional chaperone (ie. a qualified nurse).

The trainer should not only advise you of any such pitfalls, but also of the arrangements made to support the staff. (For example, I advise my trainee doctors that the nursing staff on the team have been warned to expect requests for chaperoning, and I have requested the nursing staff to take these requests seriously.) The trainer should ensure that you are quickly equipped with the absolutely essential knowledge that you need before you can see your first patient on the firm. This may involve an explanation of the clinical condition (if a subspecialty); the management of serious problems (eg. the basics of the Mental Health Act 1983, the management of violence); or a description of the political context to clinical practice (eg. any white papers from the Government indicating that practice will change). Your trainer should also make sure that you are introduced to the people with whom you will be working closely (ward manager, nurses, social workers, etc) and that you are shown around the unit. After all this, you should be ready to start seeing patients.

Supervision

Formal supervision with a trainer involves setting aside a regular time in the week. For busy people, its value is often questioned — by trainers, trainees, managers, colleagues and anyone else who would rather you did something that they regard as a greater priority in this time slot.

Such an attitude is partly the result of a misunderstanding of the purpose of supervision. Supervision is not a cosy chat with the boss. Nor, just because we are talking about trainers who are also consultant psychiatrists, is it psychotherapy. If a trainee needs psychological or psychiatric treatment, that needs to be provided elsewhere. Supervision is a regular review of the training programme. It involves monitoring progress towards the goals and identifying obstacles (many of which are simple and easily addressed) that the trainee might face in achieving his or her goals. It follows that you need to have a regular, secure, uninterrupted slot with your consultant trainer. You set the agenda for this. If you do not have a regular slot, problems that could be dealt with tend to fester and training opportunities may be missed.

In the early weeks of the attachment, you may find that you encounter clinical situations with which you are unfamiliar. While you may be advised of practical clinical steps to take in a ward round or other clinical meeting, supervision offers you the opportunity to relate what you have seen clinically to the theoretical knowledge-base for the discipline. By discussing the case with the consultant trainer from a more theoretical stance, you can address one of your main goals of the attachment — to learn about the discipline.

In supervision, you can also raise practical problems that you may be having. It may be, for example, that you cannot get your patient seen by the occupational therapist (OT). Your consultant trainer may be able to advise you of the current OT arrangements. This is an aspect of service delivery.

But the problem may be that you wish to visit another unit that your consultant trainer has suggested as a training exercise. It may be that you are uncertain how to take time away from your clinical work to undertake this training task. Your consultant trainer should be able to advise you how to solve this problem so that you do not end up missing out on an agreed training experience. Such problems are best brought up in supervision.

Supervision, in other words, is your time — your opportunity to review your training needs with your trainer. You should try to ensure that you are punctual, as you will not be able to cover as much if you are late. Your trainer should also make a special effort to be on time regularly. You should indicate (politely) to the trainer that you are very concerned if he or she does not attend, or attends late on a frequent basis. You should be aware that the trainer provides the supervision as a contractual duty, not because he or she is 'being nice'. If a consultant wishes to train junior doctors, it is an absolute requirement of the college that weekly supervision is provided.

Occasionally, the trainer or other members of the clinical team will have noticed areas in which you seem to be having difficulties. Supervision gives the trainer the opportunity to raise such concerns with you. This should be done in a sympathetic, non-confrontational way, with a view to resolution, not condemnation. None of us is perfect, and we should all try to learn from the observations of others.

We have already discussed that supervision is not psychotherapy and that its function is to facilitate your doing the job to the optimal level. However, there may be things in your personal life that are having an impact on your ability to do the job. While your personal life is private, you may need to advise your trainer of an issue that affects your job. Supervision should take place in private and you may be able to bring the issue up in confidence. You do not need to inform the supervisor of more than is absolutely essential. The trainer may, in turn, be able to offer you some practical advice; but, to reiterate, he or she will not be able to provide any form of medical or psychological treatment. If such treatment is required, your consultant trainer may be able to advise you where to seek appropriate help. Your trainer may also be your line manager, so if there is a health issue, you may be advised to go to occupational health.

Other personal issues (some serious, some less so) may need to be discussed in supervision. Many of the issues raised in *Chapter 3* have been raised, appropriately, in supervision that I have undertaken. It is simply not appropriate for a trainer to tell you, if your child is ill one day, that you should 'not let the side down'. What you need to find, if some aspect of your personal life is interfering with your work, is a compromise that gets the best for both the workplace and your home life.

Assessment and appraisal

These words often strike fear into the hearts of otherwise sensible human beings. Doctors, in particular, are usually successes of the educational system. They are used to taking exams and getting top marks. They are used to people being impressed at how clever they are. How could anyone criticise them? What do they need appraisal for? They are good doctors aren't they?

Such fears are, of course, entirely unfounded. As with the term 'supervision', fears and myths arise from a lack of understanding of what appraisal is. It is simply a review of what has happened. You will recall that at the beginning of the posting, we advised that goals should be set. The appraisal simply asks whether those goals were met. Either they were, or they weren't.

The appraisal is also an opportunity to reflect on those goals that were not achieved. They may not have been achieved because of lack of time, in which case, the trainer can learn a lesson about what can be done in a given period, and should alter his or her suggested goals to the next trainee. Or, the goals may not have been achieved because the trainee was ill for a period of time, or the trust had to ask the trainee to cover an additional post. There are a whole host of reasons why the goals might not have been achieved, either in full or to as great an extent as might have been hoped.

However, the appraisal process is not a subjective evaluation of the trainee by the trainer: it has nothing to do with whether the trainer 'likes' the trainee; it is not a grading of the trainee on the grounds of 'flair' or 'aptitude'; it does not indicate that you are clever or a 'star' performer. It simply asks if you did what you set out to do. And if the appraisal comes at the end of a period of regular supervision, there should be no surprises for either you or your trainer, because problems should have been detected along the way and dealt with. The appraisal is not an exam.

The appraisal process is better managed when we can find objective criteria on which to estimate goals. They may include the numbers of:

- new patients seen (and/or discussed with the consultant in supervision)
- follow-up patients seen
- ward rounds attended
- journal clubs attended/presented
- academic meetings attended
- case presentations made to peers
- other agencies visited.

These goals are illustrative; a whole list can be made and tailored both to the individual posting and to the rotation as a whole.

Some subjective comments can be made, such as on the nature of the interpersonal behaviour of the trainee with other staff members and with patients. But even here, specific examples should underpin a summary statement.

Problems can also be listed. They may relate to the trainee (complaints; health problems) or to the structure of the post (eg. the number of supervision sessions missed; who cancelled, and why).

A useful preparation for the appraisal is to record all data relating to the goals in a log book. This might, for example, allow the trainee to list all new patients seen as he or she goes along. At the end, the number of names can easily be added up and brought as a summary piece of data to the appraisal. Over the the course of the rotation, this can be divided up by clinical condition. Currently, normative data do not exist, but after dealing with a few trainees, most trainers will have a realistic idea of the number of patients that can be seen over a given period of time.

At the end of an appraisal in a training post, you should have a clear idea of what you have achieved and what gaps you may wish to address in the course of future training.

Audit

If you are a doctor, you presumably want to make patients better. But **do** you make patients better? 'Of course I do,' you reply. But how do you know?

The chances are, you don't know: you just **think** you know. Your mind has no doubt just wandered back to that Mrs Smith, whom you treated last week, and whom you resuscitated successfully from a cardiac arrest. Or to Mr Jones, whom you stopped from killing himself when he came to you in the A&E department last week. (If he was so intent on killing himself, why did he come to see you in A&E rather than just getting on with the job?)

In case you are getting hot under the collar, I am not being sarcastic. Of course, I realise that these were major medical successes, and that your intervention stopped one, possibly two people dying. But they probably weren't the only people you treated in the last month. What happened to the others? You can only know if you look back: only then can you think about what you did and whether your patients improved. Some will have got better. Some will be the same. Some will have got worse.

For those patients who didn't do so well, was it your fault? I don't mean this in the way lawyers and the more hostile sections of the press might mean it. I mean that you need to look at why these patients did not do so well. Maybe they were more ill than the ones who improved. Maybe they had different illnesses or prognoses. Or maybe something that you did, or did not do, contributed in some way. If so, I am not seeking to criticise you or say that you are a bad doctor. Most doctors are caring, considerate and competent people. But, we all make mistakes. The aim of looking back at the patients who did not do so well is not so we can beat ourselves up about it, but so that we can learn from our mistakes.

The process of looking back, with the aim of learning from mistakes and improving future practice, is called audit. Not so frightening, is it? And just to make it even easier, there are two types of audit in the medical world:

- medical audit – in which a **doctor** looks back at his/her own practice
- clinical audit – in which a **team** looks back at its own practice

Nowadays, most medical care is delivered by multidisciplinary teams. Most errors occur in the way that the team functions, rather than as a result of deliberate malice or incompetence on the part of any one individual.

Let's take a fictional example to illustrate how a system failure can lead to treatment failure. The doctors and nurses in the psychiatric outpatient department at Nosuch Hospital are concerned that only around 10% of patients turn up to their appointments. They know that psychiatric patients often fail to attend, but this rate seems absurdly low. So, they decide to do an audit. They find the notes of all the patients who were invited for an appointment in the past month. They find that every patient has a copy of a letter offering them the appointment they missed. Then, in the course of discussing it, someone points out that Bill who works in the post room has been off ill for the past six months. The audit team go into the post room and find a whole pile of letters that has not been sent out. No wonder the patients didn't come. The manager is informed (he had been covering two other colleagues on three sites as well as trying to do his own job, and he thought that Bill was well and at work) and immediately gets temporary cover, as he now finds out that Bill will be off for another three months. One month later, 70% of patients are turning up for their appointments.

Clearly, things can go wrong, and it may not be any one particular person's fault. But there might also be more than one reason. Note in the example above that improvement has still only reached 70% attendance. Why are the other 30% of appointments being missed? The audit process demands that we do another audit to address the remaining 30%. When a further improvement is made, we must address what is left — and so on.

Let's look at audit in a more positive way. It's asking the question: 'What is the clinical team trying to achieve, have we achieved it, and can we do even better?' The process of review is a continuous one and is referred to as the audit cycle (*Figure 2.1*).

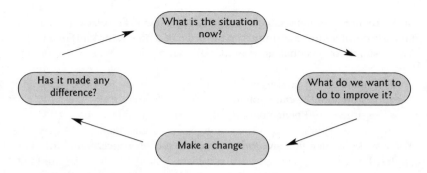

Figure 2.1: The audit cycle

If you are asked to take part in an audit, you need to clarify that you will be doing clinical audit. In this way, it is the team, not the individual, that is being looked at. Ideally, each team would look at every process that it undertakes. But this would be a very time-consuming task, and would remain so until the recordings of processes in the NHS are fully computerised. At present, many audit tasks require data to be collected by hand; consequently, current practice is that teams doing audit will take a question that interests them. It may be a question of clinical outcome (eg. how many people have we vaccinated in the past year?) or it may be a question of administrative process (eg. how many people attended the outpatient department last year?). The team evaluate their result and ask themselves how the situation could be improved. They decide on one change they will make, implement that change, and review (say, in twelve months' time) whether or not the situation has improved.

As well as the anxiety that many staff members express about the purpose of audit, it still makes demands on time and resources. The team have to decide who is going to collect the data they require and how that person's routine work will be covered. In reality, few teams currently have spare capacity to carry out the task. Some trusts have an audit team to support clinical teams, but these audit teams are usually small. As a result, access to effective audit support is patchy.

Research

Conceptually, research is simple and is just a formalised way of doing what we do every day. It is about asking what we want to know; working out how to find the answers; and finding out things that we did not know before. For example, suppose you are working out your weekly shopping. You might decide that you want to know the price of apples. You know that there are three greengrocers on your local high street. The obvious research task is to visit all three and find out the price of a pound (or kilo) of apples. You visit all three shops and note the following prices:

- store A: 90 pence/pound
- store B: 91 pence/pound
- store C: 90 pence/pound

You now know that you are going to have to pay 90 pence/pound for your apples. It is research because until you visited the three shops you did not know what the prices would be. Of course, if your nextdoor neighbour had just been to the three shops and found out the prices, you wouldn't bother to do it yourself. Before you went, you might have taken the precaution of knocking on your neighbour's door to check that he or she hadn't just come back from the shops.

Medical (and psychiatric) research is no different. It is about asking what we don't know and how we can find it out. This has been formalised into seven steps:

1. Find out what it is you want to know (ie. define the research question).
2. Find out if anyone has already discovered the answer to what you want to know (ie. search the literature to find if anyone else has done a study that answers your question).
3. If nobody has done this research before, decide how you are going to do it. You should do this in writing for two reasons: first, it will focus and clarify your mind; second, others can read what you are planning and may be able to give you advice on how to do it better (eg. in our example with the price of apples, a neighbour might have suggested that you just telephone the shops rather than visit them). The formal document in which you write down your plans is called a research protocol.
4. Find out how much your research will cost, and how you would meet that cost. In the apples example, our visit to the high street may have taken fifteen minutes. Did you have fifteen minutes to spare that day? If you would rather have used the telephone, did you have one? Could someone else have gone for you? Would you have had to pay them for it? Similarly, you may need to pay for the time of a psychiatric research registrar, a statistician, nurses, pharmacists and a secretary; you may also need to buy a computer. Where will the money come from? Joining a research group is one way of pooling skills and resources.

5. Having clarified what you want to do, you must ensure that it is ethical. In our example, your neighbour might have the data on his home computer. But breaking and entering when he is out would not be an ethical way of getting the price of apples. Medical research is occasionally carried out without thought to the comfort of patients. In some early studies, patients were, frankly, abused by doctors in the name of research. To protect patients, research ethics committees have been developed to assess plans in the research protocol. They should be asked to review the proposed research to confirm it is ethical.

6. You now need to do your research: collect the information that you set out to collect, and analyse it. If your project was properly designed and carried out, you will now have some answers.

7. Others may also want to know the outcome of your research. So tell them – at a learned conference, for example, or by publication in a journal.

Examinations

Postgraduate medical examinations will introduce many of the candidates to a number of new experiences. Before a doctor can enter the examination for the MRCPsych, he or she must demonstrate to the college that he or she has had the requisite training (one year of psychiatry for Part I; three and a half years of psychiatry on a recognised training scheme for the final exam). But, unlike the initial medical school degree, the MRCPsych examination is not confirmation that the scheme has trained the candidate to the required standard. Furthermore, the increased emphasis on the clinical component of the examination means that performance anxiety can influence the outcome. Many previous high-flyers will have their first experience of failing an exam.

But whether you are destined to sail through or have a few hiccups on the way, you should not forget the claim of the Royal College of Psychiatrists Examinations Committee that, whichever way you test candidates, the better ones end up coming through. You should not be put off by the process. You simply need a few additional skills.

The first, and most obvious, is that you have to learn how to give a performance on the day. Doctors are not actors, but when you come to examinations, you have to learn a few acting skills. Second, you have to learn not to fear failure. If you get through both parts of the examination on the first sitting, well done. But remember that some excellent clinicians have impressed the examiners so greatly that they were invited to present themselves again. Getting the MRCPsych is not like a school examination; it is not graded. It is simply a matter of pass or fail. Unless you are going to win the Gaskell Prize for coming top, it is no more than an irritating but necessary step on your path to becoming a consultant. As with any other task on the route to a higher goal, you must prepare yourself properly.

How can you do this? Ideally, the rotation you are on will be organised so that you automatically cover all the tasks you need — including exam preparation — in the course of your time on it. In reality, however, this may not happen, so let's consider what the exam is, and how you can prepare for it.

The aim of the MRCPsych examination is to determine whether or not the candidate is clinically competent in psychiatric practice and has the essential elements of the numerous different branches (epidemiology, pharmacology, psychology, genetics, sociology, neurology, molecular biology, statistics, philosophy, law, etc) of scientific and other knowledge necessary to make clinical decisions and offer advice.

You need to gain clinical experience of the range of psychiatric conditions (listed in *ICD-10* or *DSM-IV* and roughly equivalent to those mentioned in *Chapter 1*) and to know the scientific underpinning for psychiatric practice. The syllabus is set out in the Royal College of Psychiatrists document on the curriculum for the MRCPsych (for details see *Chapter 6*). It is a very long and comprehensive document, but you should not be put off by it. You will not be able to cover everything in it in detail. However, if you are familiar with the contents, you will find that you pay greater attention to particularly relevant bits of information as you come across them and are therefore likely to remember them better.

In terms of getting clinical experience, as long as you do jobs in all three branches (child, adult and old age psychiatry), you are likely to get adequate exposure to patients with the range of common psychiatric conditions. Make sure, however, that you do not spend an undue proportion of your training time in specialist units, especially if turnover of patients is low. Your aim for the MRCPsych is to get a good grounding in bread-and-butter aspects of psychiatry. You can follow up specialist interests after you have passed the exam, either in a research job or in your SpR training. At the SHO level, do not look down on the jobs in the district general hospitals: they provide you with an excellent opportunity to gain solid clinical experience.

Although you are primarily providing medical care, you should remember that every patient that you see as a junior doctor is a case study for you. You should try to make a conscious effort to remember the patients you have seen and ensure that you have seen several patients with each of the main psychiatric conditions (although this list is not exhaustive):

- Down's syndrome
- autism
- conduct disorder
- enuresis/encopresis
- school refusal
- schizophrenia
- manic-depressive illness (in both hypomanic and depressive phases)
- obsessive compulsive disorder
- social phobia
- anxiety disorders
- anorexia nervosa
- bulimia nervosa
- alcohol dependence
- opiate dependence
- benzodiazepine dependence
- puerperal mental illness
- somatic presentations of psychological distress and liaison psychiatric patients
- patients in a forensic setting
- senile dementia of the Alzheimer's type
- depression in the elderly.

You may wish to list the patients you have seen with these conditions in your log book for the whole rotation so that when you read about the conditions, you can relate the theoretical knowledge to the clinical picture you have seen. You should also make a mental note of the different scenarios that you encounter. By recalling what you (or a senior colleague) did in a given situation, you will be better equipped to give a meaningful answer in the parts of the clinical examination that present you with specific clinical dilemmas.

But you will not get the best out of your rotation unless you are well-versed in the essential psychiatric clinical skills. The first books you must read in the first few days of your first job, if not before you start (time permitting), are:

✻ A book describing how to examine a psychiatric patient thoroughly (such as the Maudsley orange book or Leff and Isaacs; for details see *Chapter 6*).
✻ A book describing the range of psychiatric symptoms (Fish's *Psychopathology* or Sim's *Symptoms in the Mind*; see *Chapter 6*).

Once you have read these books, you must always examine patients in detail. It will be time-consuming and at first you will feel under pressure, but if you do not examine your patients properly and discuss them with your senior colleagues, you will not develop an understanding of the difference between psychiatric care by a professional and vague support by a well-meaning lay person. No-one needs to pay the fee for psychiatric care if all they get is a nice, but therapeutically irrelevant, chat.

Making sure that you examine your patients thoroughly, especially in your first job, is one of the few training tasks that, if need be, you should stay late for. Getting the background information is, in some ways, harder. In the first instance, you should try to read a psychiatric textbook as quickly as you can. Choose one of moderate length, such as the *Oxford Textbook of Psychiatry*, which you can get through with a fair degree of speed. The purpose is to get a quick overview of the subject and an introduction to some of the important concepts. You can go for the giant textbooks (eg. Kaplan and Sadock), but they give a lot of detail and you can get bogged down. You can return to them later when you have a greater knowledge-base, or when you are trying to get greater depth in one topic.

However, textbooks are not always well-written or well-edited. They may not have enough detail for your needs; they may be over-long and verbose; or they may contain only those parts of the topic that interested the writer of that chapter, rather than a full and balanced overview of the topic. The result is that, while a textbook is a good starting place, it is rarely sufficient. It seldom repays the large sum invested in it, and you should think carefully whether you really need to own anything more than a moderate-sized textbook. The larger ones can be found in the library.

You are going to need to enlarge your knowledge by reading articles in the learned journals. You should be aware that the general medical journals; *British Medical Journal, The Lancet, Journal of the American Medical Association, New England Journal of Medicine, Canadian Medical Association Journal, Medical Journal of Australia* – publish many articles in the field of mental illness. From time to time, they publish update reviews of various mental illnesses, such as schizophrenia, bipolar disorder, obsessive-compulsive disorder, eating disorder, alcohol-dependence syndrome and psychopharmacology.

You should also be aware of the specialist journals, such as the *British Journal of Psychiatry* (which is sent to inceptors of the Royal College, ie. trainees who have applied for it), *American Journal of Psychiatry* and *Archives of General Psychiatry*. Bear in mind that, at the start of your training, the articles published in these journals may be too detailed. But as you get past Part I, you should be reading every month the abstracts of articles in journals such as these in order to gain an idea of recent developments in the field. The Royal College of Psychiatrists also publishes a training journal, suitable for both trainees and fully trained staff doing continuing professional development, entitled *Advances in Psychiatric Treatment*.

The cost of subscriptions to all these journals is high and if you do subscribe you quickly end up with a mountain of paper to store. The recent developments in information technology mean that if you have access to a computer and the internet — and suitable storage materials, such as recordable CDs — you can gain access to these journals easily. A particularly interesting development is the way that the NHS has obtained bulk access to online versions of several journals for its staff. You should contact the local librarian for free access. In London, the development of KA24, which allows access to the OVID journal database and a range of other articles, is available via a web page (www.hilo.nhs.uk).

To complete your access to professional knowledge, you should be aware of the PubMed website (medline; www.ncbi.nlm.nih.gov), where a vast range of journals can be searched for relevant articles and abstracts. Other professional databases such as PsychLit and PsychInfo are relevant to psychiatric practice. You will need to use them if you are researching a topic in detail.

These sort of knowledge sources will give you enough information for the purpose of the examination. If you want to be a better doctor, you will want to know not just the technical detail and your observations in clinical practice, but also gain some idea of what a patient with a disorder suffers. The literature is full of articles of people describing their experiences of various illnesses. A selection of references is included in *Chapter 6*.

Educational opportunities and study leave

You should have access to a wide range of educational opportunities on the rotation. Some rotations will have an administrative officer who will collate information about all academic activities on all sites of the rotation and disseminate it. Typical on-site activities include journal clubs, case conferences and academic lectures. Other activities may be carried out centrally. You can also attend a variety of external conferences and courses.

A journal club is a weekly meeting of a group of professionals in which one presents an article from a professional source. In the medical sphere, it may consist of a group of psychiatric trainees or a multidisciplinary clinical team or any other self-selected group of professionals. Typically, the members of the team take it in turns to select a paper and present a summary of its contents to the rest of the group. The issues raised by the paper can also be discussed. The paper may be a recent paper from a medical, nursing or social-work journal, or any other paper relating to the work of the group. Occasionally, a video may be shown, either one that features a recently televised programme, or one that has been bought commercially. The aim is to increase the team's awareness and knowledge of their subject.

A case conference, for academic purposes, involves a group of staff meeting, with one person presenting the medical history of a patient (with the patient's consent). The patient may even agree to attend the meeting, so that other members of staff, who may not be involved in the patient's care, may learn from the issues raised.

A wide variety of academic lectures may be available throughout the rotation. Some will relate to the medical discipline in which you are working, others will be on topics that are not related to current psychiatric discipline — but are relevant to a psychiatric trainee.

Each site, and sometimes the rotation centrally, will probably have one half-day per week that is designated as the academic morning or afternoon. It will be up to you and your consultant trainer to agree what sessions you may attend on a regular basis. The team may be accustomed to an established academic slot for your post and you will have to explain your reasons if you wish to deviate from this.

There is a requirement for MRCPsych trainees to gain experience in psychotherapeutic techniques. Typically, a candidate for the exam is expected to have treated one patient with psychotherapy for one year under supervision and one patient with cognitive-behavioural treatment over an eight-week period (or so), again under supervision. Trainees gaining such experience are usually expected to attend a weekly psychotherapy supervision session, where the progress of their patients can be discussed.

In addition, you may wish to attend an educational course. Some might be available locally and relate to an additional skill, such as a one-day course on a computer software programme (such as Microsoft Word or PowerPoint) that may be provided through the library or some other local mechanism. Other courses may be related to an aspect of training that is clinically relevant across a number of clinical disciplines, such as a course on restraint techniques to handle violent incidents or the workings of the UK Mental Health Act.

Finally, there are courses specifically designed to prepare candidates for the MRCPsych examination. The rotation may have its own course and you may be expected to attend this course. There are also commercial courses, either on weekends or for longer periods of time, which are advertised through the medical press. Certain organisations provide training courses for MRCPsych trainees without the exams being specifically exam-directed. For example, the British Association for

Psychopharmacology organises a diploma course in this discipline.

There are a wide range of medical conferences and sometimes trainees are invited by their trainer to attend. The Royal College of Psychiatrists organises an annual conference; the sections of the College organise their own specialist conferences.

In addition to all of the above, there may be a number of informal teaching and training sessions available, specially preparing for the exam. Trainees may also be invited by their consultant trainer to accompany them to certain clinical experiences as a training exercise. You should listen out, particularly in the early stages of your training, in case your consultant trainer is making a visit to see a patient in a prison, and ask if you can accompany him or her.

With such a bewildering array of options, it is clearly up to each trainee to work out which sessions he or she will attend. It is wise to keep an overview of the type of training exercises that you have undertaken in one central place, such as in the log book for the rotation. Then, in conjunction with either your current consultant trainer or with the clinical tutor or course organiser, you can review progress and ascertain gaps in your training that you wish to address at some future stage.

With the availability of so many training opportunities, you and your colleagues are left with the question of how the time is to be found for you to attend while doing a full-time job, and where funding will come from for the courses you wish to attend. It is worth recalling at this stage that your training is included in your contract. Being allowed time away from your routine work to gain this training is not a favour – it is a contractual right. Of course, if you are going to assert your right to training sessions, you must do so in a reasonable manner. You must make sure that adequate arrangements are made to cover you in your absence, and that it is convenient to your firm to manage without you. You cannot just disappear on a training course without giving your work colleagues notice.

Similarly, there will be (usually a standard) contractual amount of study leave available to you. You can request an amount of time up to the limit, but you cannot assume that you will be granted more than this. Nowadays, many rotations set aside a budget to pay for courses. To ensure that this is applied fairly, each trainee may be allocated a certain amount per year.

You should not feel guilty about taking your study leave, as it is your contractual right. If you have applied to go on a course and have given a reasonable period of notice to the team (a matter of several weeks), then it is the responsibility of the team manager, not you, to ensure that the cover needed is in place.

Contracts, however, are only intended to clarify minimum

entitlements. Many places are considerably more generous. Typically, you may be entitled to twenty-five days study leave per year. Some rotations will insist that regular half-day attendance at the local MRCPsych course should be deducted from this allowance; others will not. Local journal clubs and academic meetings are usually not deducted from the study leave allowance. Conversely, certain events take place outside the working day; this is growing less common, but you should be cautious before deciding that you will not attend a regular training event set for 5.15pm once a week.

You should find out early on the rotation what the arrangements are and the mechanism of obtaining suitable leave. You could even try to find out from present trainees if there are any problems in getting study leave before you apply for the rotation.

Preparing for the exam

Your preparation for both Part I and Part II of the MRCPsych starts on the day you enter your first hospital for your first job in psychiatry. You will need to gain the clinical basis that we mentioned earlier – how to examine a patient, etc – as quickly as you can, in order to practice. If you do this properly, you will realise that the clinical part of the exam is no different from your daily routine, apart from the fact that you may have to cut corners in the exam because of the time restriction. In the exam, if there is truly more material than is possible to obtain in the course of the hour or so that you are with the patient, you can always tell the examiner what you would have done had you had more time.

So — even before you start your formal preparation for the exam, you should try to develop good habits early on. Examine carefully and, over time, learn which parts can be hurried or abbreviated for the exam. Also, start reading about the psychiatric illnesses early in order to build on what you learn. This will give you more time to build up your knowledge base.

When the time comes to take the exam, you must be sure not only of the syllabus, but of the way that the examination is organised. At present, the Royal College of Psychiatrists requires a multiple choice questionnaire paper (MCQ) and an objective clinical structured examination (OSCE; for those who pass the MCQ) for Part I and two MCQ papers, a critical review paper, an essay paper, plus two clinical examinations: an individual patient assessment and a set of patient management problems ('vignettes') examination. You can find details and examples on the College website.

No doubt, you will not need reminding that you should practice past papers as much as you can. There are also now a wide range of books specifically targeted for the MRCPsych.

One word of caution in your preparation: if you are practising MCQs, do not simply go through a list of questions and decide your answer. Try to look up what the correct answer is in a textbook or other source, so that you can be sure. It is not unheard of for some of the 'answers' in some of the MCQ textbooks to be incorrect.

Many people find it helpful to study in groups. Find some colleagues who are also taking the exam at the same time as you and see if you are all willing to meet up to discuss tactics and progress on a regular basis, and to support each other during this stressful time. Many rotations contain consultants and specialist registrars who are only too willing to give informal help to candidates preparing for the exam; to listen to cases; to practise vignettes; or to practise examining. It is not a bad idea to accept the offer of more than one senior, as their different styles and emphases will be mirrored by the different type of examiner you can expect.

However prepared you are, the exam will always be stressful. While different people approach the examination in different ways, if you are able to get the bulk of your factual learning in early, you can spend the time near the exam revising. Many people find that, as the exam approaches, they become increasingly anxious (inevitably) and learning new information at this stage is difficult. You might well want to concentrate on reducing the pressure on yourself (ensuring adequate rest, proper diet, some diversion —exercise, walks, TV) in the days immediately before the examination.

Taking the examination

After you have submitted your entry form, with your consultant trainer and clinical tutor sponsoring you, you will be sent details of where you should go for the written papers. You should ensure that you prepare carefully for the practicalities — where the exam is, how to get there, what time it starts. These details should be sorted out well in advance. On the day itself, ensure that you give yourself plenty of time for the journey, allowing for the possibility of unavoidable delays (traffic, problems with trains, etc). When you hear that you are being invited for the clinical part of the examination, you should prepare for this day with equal care.

At those stages of presenting to examiners in person (ie. especially the individual patient assessment and the patient management problems), you should, as a rule of thumb, bear in mind that you are not trying to show the examiners that you are a genius, but that you are someone who is competent in the basics of clinical psychiatry and that you are the sort of person who the consultants examining you would be happy to have as colleagues (or at least as their specialist registrar). They want to know that you can assess a patient and discuss the case with them as one colleague to another. From the patient management problems, they want to know that you have seen a patient or two in your three and a half years; that you have some experience to draw on; and that, if faced with an unusual situation, to which there may be no correct answer to the clinical problem, you will handle the situation in a safe and competent manner.

Of course, in the formal situation of the examination, it is hard to be relaxed with the examiners, but they are not trying to catch you out. Recall some of the conversations you have had with your consultant colleagues in the course of your training. Apart from the fact that, in the exam, you are not allowed to ask the senior colleague (ie. the examiner) for his or her opinion, the level of discussion should be similar to that which you would have with a clinical colleague back in the unit.

Dress as though you are a professional psychiatrist, attend on time, and speak the language of psychiatry in an appropriate manner. It is helpful if you can refer to the literature in your discussion, but you do not need to have the reference in full — it is acceptable to refer to 'the article in last month's *British Journal of Psychiatry*' and describe the article to show you have read it. Do not make up references, as your examiners will probably be aware that you are doing this. You can prepare by making a habit of reading the abstracts of the main journals (*British Journal of Psychiatry*, *American Journal of Psychiatry* and *Archives of General Psychiatry* and psychiatric articles in the main general medical journals, such as *The Lancet*) on a regular basis for several months before the exam.

When seeing patients in the examination, always behave professionally. This means taking control of the interview, while showing courtesy and compassion. In the individual patient assessment, you can quickly get to the issue by asking the patient for the details of the diagnosis and the medication they are taking. (If the patient refuses to tell you the diagnosis, it is entirely legitimate to say that in this exam your task is to either agree or disagree with the diagnosis that the doctors treating the patient have given. So they can tell you what other doctors think they have got.) From this, you should be in the ball park of what clinical picture you are dealing with, and you can ask your questions accordingly.

In terms of the sorts of cases you are likely to see, you should appreciate that the process of obtaining patients for the examination determines who you will see. The responsible consultant for the examination centre will ask colleagues for suitable cases: not only patients with symptoms and hopefully signs, but also patients whose conditions are chronic and stable. Occasionally, someone with an acute presentation will be available, but this is more a matter of luck for the examination centre on the day. So, you will get a typical case that the centre can get their hands on easily — people with the common and bread-and-butter conditions (schizophrenia, bipolar disorder, alcoholism, obsessive-compulsive disorder, learning disabilities, childhood depression, etc). There may be more than one pathology.

Also, be aware that, although the examiners only see you in the exam room, there are a number of people who see you on the way in to when you leave — supporting doctors, administrators, etc. They will be able to advise of any impropriety, so do remain in examination mode until you have left the hospital premises.

Reviewing progress on the rotation

On a good rotation, you should have regular meetings with the clinical tutor to review your overall progress. The purpose of these meetings is to ensure that you are enjoying the rotation and that you still seem to be suitable to be a psychiatrist (on a SHO rotation) or consultant (on an SpR rotation). The importance of these meetings is not to receive a pat on the head, but to ensure that you are getting an appropriate training for the goals that you have in mind.

In an SHO rotation, you need to be sure that you are getting introductory exposure to all the branches of psychiatry. In an SpR rotation, you should have some idea of what sort of a consultant you wish to be; what gaps you have in your training (both clinical and managerial); and how you will plug those gaps. Although trainees often seek a 'nice' consultant (ideally, all consultants will behave in a kindly but professional manner with their trainees), you should seek postings with consultants who can teach you or give you clinical experience in areas with which you are unfamiliar, or which will plug a significant gap in your knowledge. A written record of your progress and postings is always helpful, as it can form the basis of identifying the gaps in your training.

Progression up the ladder

At the time of writing, there is still an overall shortage of consultant psychiatrists. Assuming that you pass the MRCPsych (eventually), you are likely to be able to get an SpR place without undue difficulty. Some choose the period immediately after the MRCPsych to spend a year in a research position. While getting publications is always helpful, high-flying original research is not essential for a consultant position. In the SpR grade, you may be able to undertake some research, but what you can achieve one day a week over three years is very limited.

There are different views about the selection of the SpR rotation. Some feel that there is value in staying in the same geographical location, as a consultant who has been an SHO and SpR in one place will know the local system well and be well-equipped to start life as a consultant in a familiar environment. Others see the SpR grade as an opportunity to widen their experience, and there is something to be said for going to another geographical location to that of the SHO rotation, as it is instructive to see a range of people do things differently.

As I have said throughout this chapter, your choice of clinical placement should be made in the context of your life choices, not vice versa.

3

Putting your career in the context of the rest of your life

You may wonder why on earth you need to read a chapter like this. You're a qualified doctor, you have plenty of experience — and you know what's what. Why would you need someone to tell you how to live your life?

Twenty years ago, you could still find a doctors' mess in many hospitals. Some had bars and some provided meals, such as breakfast.

But the days of pampering 'elite' doctors are well gone. The backlash, which has led doctors to be seen as excessively privileged hospital workers, has caused the pendulum to swing to the other extreme — hospitals now do as little as possible for their doctors. Doctors are expected to work for twenty-four hours a day, for several days at a time on occasions. But it is regarded as 'pampering' to ensure that food is available for them. Even if you have been working for twenty hours continuously — and you may only get a few minutes' rest in the on-call room in the early hours of the morning before the bleep goes off summoning you to another several hours work — you are still expected to make your own bed if you want to lie down. For those of you who think that this picture is an exaggeration (because you have not experienced it), be under no illusion that it is not.

The purpose of describing this bygone era, and the changes in the way doctors are viewed by the general public, is not to complain about the abuse that doctors have accepted more recently: it is to make a more important point about the medical workplace. Years ago, hospitals were communities; they would be relatively self-contained and people working there would know each other and support each other. Although workers nowadays are able to make some working relationships — even friendships — with colleagues, the vastness of the organisations and the constant changes of personnel mean that hospitals are no longer organisations filled with mutually supportive staff.

In the past, you could take up a career as a doctor, nurse or ancillary worker and, in effect, you would be looked after for life. Some staff would live in hospital accommodation on site; others would have friends and mentors who could guide them through life's travails. Even if the picture was never quite as rosy as I am painting it, the demands of the outside world on all hospital staff have increased greatly in recent years. Hospital staff are seen now as workers who are responsible for turning up at work, then going home. When resources are scarce, they are not given priority, even if this impairs their ability to carry out their jobs. For example, very few hospital doctors (let alone other staff) can expect a reserved parking space at the hospital for their car. This is not a matter of privilege. Many doctors are expected to carry out clinics on different sites on the same day. Taxis between sites are rarely provided, and if the doctor drives between different sites to attend clinics, he or she may not be able to park at the second clinic. There was even a story in the newspapers recently about a consultant who had to cancel an outpatient clinic because he had spent over an hour looking for somewhere to park, without success. (This is an extraordinary example of management failure, but that's for discussion elsewhere.) What it means is that doctors and other healthcare staff are no more immune to the problems of 'work-life balance' than are workers in other sectors of the economy.

In the course of your career, you will need to have somewhere to live. You will have some leisure time and activities. You may have one or several personal relationships. You may get married. You may have children. You will get older and, either as a result of age, personal accident or illness, you may have to work with a chronic disability or condition. You may have others in your personal social network, such as ageing parents, who make demands on you. And at some time, as happens to us all, you will suffer bereavement. You have to cope with all this while carrying out a full-time job.

In the course of supervising a wide variety of colleagues, the pressures of the outside world have often been raised as issues. Of course, it is not the job of a supervisor to sort out personal problems (see *Chapter 2*), but a line manager should be aware of personal issues that affect a worker's ability to carry out his or her job satisfactorily. For example, if a parent is only able to work if he or she leaves a child with a childminder, there may be times when the staff member is suddenly unable to attend on a given day, because the childminder is off work through sickness, holiday, bereavement (or something else). The manager will need to be able to make changes in the service to accommodate the worker being diverted from his or her task by such an outside pressure. If it occurs frequently, the manager will need to discuss it with the worker. For example, if a childminder leaves, the worker may bring the impending additional demand to the attention of the manager. The manager cannot solve the problem for the worker, but may be able to offer a few informal pointers.

This, therefore, is the point of this chapter. I will go through a number of common problems that occur to doctors (and others) at different stages of their careers. Some of them may never apply to you, but others will. As with the colleagues I have supervised, I cannot give you formal, professional advice (I am not a financial adviser, building expert, etc). But there are some common basic practical points that may start you off in the right direction.

One word of caution. Much of what you read in this chapter may be dull or seem a statement of the downright obvious. If so, good for you — because you are well-equipped to deal with life's challenges. But the chances are that there are one or two problem areas for even the best of us. Sometimes, we forget the most obvious steps and then wonder why we can't get ourselves out of a fix.

Life choices

Life, as they say, is not a rehearsal. If there is something that you really want to do, and you don't do it now, you may not get to do it at all. For example, if you are doing a job you don't like, don't carry on doing it — unless it is a clear, time-limited step to a higher goal that you have set yourself.

In other words, if you are working unhappily in a job without a clear career progression, hoping vaguely that some day something might change if you wait long enough, then you should reconsider. The fantasised improvement probably won't happen.

But if you are an SHO or an SpR on a rotation, and you have decided that you want to be a consultant, there may be some posts that you do not enjoy as much as others – but which you have to complete as part of your training.

What is always important is that you should constantly be thinking about what you are doing and deciding if everything is going as it should. Not only is this important in jobs you don't like, but also in jobs that you are enjoying. In the latter, you should make sure that you remain focused on what you intended to get out of the job. If you are doing a job in a firm where your colleagues are fun, but then take all the interesting patients, you may feel when you look back that you had an enjoyable six months, but that you did not learn as much as you could have done.

So, you have choices. But you should not allow yourself to be taken in by the casual use of language that sometimes occurs in respect of choices and rights. People can claim to have the right to free choice, but in real life the range of choices is always limited. If you decide to leave an SHO post in psychiatry, you cannot apply for a job as a partner in a law firm if you have not had a legal training and the requisite expertise. Nor can you go around the world as a guest on a luxury yacht if you don't own one (or have the money to buy one) and don't have a friend who does. And one of the problems of choice is that the options available may all have drawbacks.

Another problem with choice is that there are always consequences. If you are in a shop and you have enough money to buy either a radio or a camera, but not both, then once you have chosen one, you cannot have the other. Economists refer to this as 'opportunity cost'. It also occurs with all other resources, including time. If you choose to do a job for six months in general psychiatry, then you cannot get the six months back and say that you would rather have spent that six-month period doing a job in dermatology (or travelling around the world).

As well as losses, there are other types of consequence. Choice changes the world irreversibly. If, for example, you are married and you choose to commit adultery (and your spouse finds out), you cannot return to an earlier stage of innocence. You are, irreversibly, an unfaithful spouse to that partner. Choices always need to be taken with consideration and care. If the consequences are serious and hard to rectify, then you should allow plenty of time before making a decision.

Having said that, the only true judge of your choices is you. Other people may not agree with your choices. But only you can decide if the choice you made led to the outcome you wanted. Your parents may want you to live in a given geographical area or marry a particular person; your friends may want you to accompany them on some trip; your employer may want you to undertake a particular piece of additional work for additional pay. But only you can decide and (especially if you disagree with them), only you can judge whether your decision was the right one.

And the big choices — career, partner (if any), accommodation, finances — are yours alone. Some of the comments that are made in the rest of this chapter should be seen as no more than suggestions. For example, it is recommended here that you would find it hard to manage a mortgage if you borrowed more than two-and-a-half times your annual salary. But you may decide to borrow five times your annual salary, live in a property you cannot afford for six months, before selling it and finding yourself broke. If you do this, you may reflect and say that you were unwise to borrow so much and that you had a bad time trying to keep the house. Alternatively, you may say that it was worth it to live in such a lovely house for six months, even if 'all good things must come to an end'. The decision as to whether you did the right thing is yours, not your mum's, your nan's, your great uncle's, the vicar's. Yours.

Which means one further thing: if you made a choice that had some clear consequence, then make the mental step of accepting that this consequence happened. If you decided to commit adultery and your spouse subsequently left you, saying your adultery was the final straw, you should accept that your choice got you where you are now and live with it.

You may say at this point that you have to make a whole range of choices for which you cannot possibly know the outcome. Often, it is only when we have done something that we have enough information to make the original choice. For example, it is only when you have done a job for a certain amount of time that you know enough about the job to know if you wanted to do it in the first place. And it may only be at that stage that you decide that you didn't want it after all. Of course (as your friends will gleefully tell you) you could have checked it out beforehand. But there is only so much time in the day and you can only speak to so many people. The balance between checking something out to the nth degree (with delay, a cost in the form of time, in making the choice) and getting on and making the choice is a judgement — again, one that only you can make. Life is not always easy, straightforward or fair.

Personal finance

As you might anticipate, I have to start this section by reminding you that I am not a financial adviser. Having said that, some of the suggestions I am about to make might help you think about your personal finances.

The first suggestion is that there is no such thing as earning money.

Now, I wouldn't take that last sentence and throw it at a tax inspector as justification for not paying your income tax. Nor would I state it boldly at a dinner party of accountants and economists and expect them to look at you as though you were a genius (a madman, yes, but not a genius).

The point I am making is that we get money either because someone gives it to us or because we take it from them. We either get it in the form of money or in the form of goods (eg. a TV) or services (eg. a haircut). When you were growing up, your parents gave you food. They did not sell it to you or ask you for the money that they had spent to buy it for you. As you got older, they may have given you pocket money. If you came from a wealthy family, they may even have given you large amounts of money to buy what you wanted – perhaps while family were alive, or in the form of an inheritance from Aunt Maud. And then you can marry someone who has money, though nowadays it seems to be watered down to having sex with them for money. I am not implying that cohabiting (or even marriage) is the same as prostitution, but from a financial point of view, if a person gives another person money following a sexual act or a sexual relationship, it makes no difference if the sum of money is the same. Indeed, in our society, people give others money simply because they like them or are sympathetic to them. The cult of celebrity, with people being paid amounts of money simply to be there (celebrities opening a fair, etc), and charities, work on the principle that you can get people to give you money because they like you. But before you get on your high horse about such frivolous ways of earning a living, remember that when you go for a job interview you aim to make the people on the panel like you (in preference to the other candidates), so that they will give you the job – and the money that goes with it.

You could beg for money; no doubt someone would give you some. You can do errands in the expectation that someone will give you money. You can give somebody specific goods in return for money (though they still have to hand the money over). It is possible to obtain something like a TV on credit and then fail to hand over the money. Some firms may be so big that they fail to come back to you when you do not hand over the money. Or you can walk out of the shop without paying (by mistake) and the shopkeeper fails to come after you (by mistake). You can do a service for someone (such as cutting their hair or repair their inguinal hernia), but they still have to hand the money over before you have it.

The NHS is a good example of how people quite legitimately take money (in the form of services) from each other. The NHS is paid for by taxation. The Government takes money from A (taxpayer), uses it to pay B (surgeon), who operates on C (patient). The effect is no different than if C had taken money from A to pay for the operation. The social mechanism of the NHS makes this process entirely acceptable.

And some people (not you or I, of course) will simply take money directly from others – stealing it. They may even make threats to ensure that the victim hands it over. Of course, in commerce, the majority of customers hand over the money they agreed in return for the goods, and the providers of goods and services have a whole set of mechanisms to ensure that they do actually get the money.

Now, let me make it clear that I do not approve of those mechanisms of taking money from other people that involve dishonesty or deceit. The purpose of this description is to try to understand more accurately how money works (in a moral-free sense), as this allows us to question (as we will in a moment) certain assumptions that many people make.

But what about earning money? In many parts of society, there are tasks that need to be done on a regular basis. Goods need to be made (eg. in a factory) before they can be sold; services need to be provided. And many of these goods (eg. TVs, washing machines, pencils, garden chairs, lavatory chains) and services (eg. fire service, dry cleaning, hairdressing, plumbing, hotel reception) have to be provided on a regular basis. It makes sense for the providers to employ a number of people. The employer agrees to pay the employee (usually on a time basis) for the work provided.

But the rate of payment will usually be as low as the employer can make it and as high as the employee can get. There is no 'right' rate for the job. The concept of a rate arises from the fact that certain services are provided so commonly that people across a large area (a town, a country) know that if they pay below a certain rate, no-one will be prepared to do the job — and that, above a certain rate, they will be spoilt for choice from equally competent applicants. But this may vary as circumstances change. In an organisation like the NHS, the use of a standard rate of pay across the country is intended to ensure that services are similar across the country (and that staff doing similar jobs co-operate with each other).

But even there, the contract of employment is only as good as the willingness of the two sides to honour their part of the bargain. An employee may have a contract saying he or she will be paid so many pounds for the week's work. The employee may carry out that work. The employer may agree that he or she owes the employee the money. But, if the employer does not have the money at the end of the week (because of 'cashflow' problems), the employee may still not receive the money. And, if the firm goes bust, with no money left to pay the people it owes, the employees may never receive the money for the work that they have done.

'So what?', you ask. Well, if earning depends on the willingness (or ability) of the employer to hand over money, then the price for the job does not need to be standard. The part of the medical profession providing services in the NHS in the UK has allowed itself to be held over a barrel by its insistence that it will provide a service, almost whatever. When the employer (the Government) has limited the amount available, and doctors have continued to work for the NHS, the price for medical labour has gone down.

Now, this is not a political treatise — and certainly not an attack on the NHS. It is to illustrate the process of how an individual doctor can end up being paid what he or she may consider an inadequate salary. This process is no different from that of any other large group of workers in the economy. But if we follow the logic through, we can deal with a major source of discontent for doctors – a relatively low salary. Doctors (like other workers) can realise from the analysis of how money is earned that they have two main options:

- to leave the NHS, blaming the low pay (and blaming the Government for lack of provision of sufficient doctors)
- to provide less of a service for the capped amount of money coming to them.

If the doctors working in the NHS choose not to take one of these options (eg. acting on the ideal of providing service whatever), they are making a choice. If you make such a choice, you must accept responsibility for the consequences. And accepting the consequences of your choice is always easier if you know that there are other options (even if they are also far from perfect).

But the way the system works currently, the impression of workers earning money is maintained. At the present time, doctors working in the NHS receive a fixed amount of money at regular intervals (eg. a monthly salary) for whatever they do in the previous time period. In the private sector, the rate for the individual will be the amount at which patients will come to him minus his expenses. This may be variable in a small practice, but in an established practice, the practitioner may experience a fixed amount of money in a fixed amount of time (eg. if a practitioner charges £200 per hour for eight hours a day, and the clinic is always full with patients who pay on time, then the practitioner will earn a regular £1600 per day).

At the present time, the NHS is, for the most part, a reliable employer. Unlike in commerce, where firms may delay payment (sometimes deliberately) to an individual or another firm, the NHS does tend to pay its workers on time. Staff take it for granted that they will receive the money that they are contractually owed. But as with all organisations, things can change over time, and even in a relatively secure organisation such as the NHS, staff need to be prepared to think about the possibility of changes to pay, conditions and pensions, and to evaluate what is best for them individually by comparing the alternative choices of employment.

The computer industry illustrates well the different types of employment. Many workers have (up until a recent change in the law) found that they could earn more money by working independently and obtaining a contract for a specified piece of work for a company than being direct employees of the company. Along with the higher payments came diminished job security, because while those who were employed had a constant, regular flow of money (assuming their employers were solvent and honest), the contract workers never knew if there was going to be another contract after the present one. For a time, there was a demand for contract workers, so the risk of being one was not high. That has changed, and it is now better to be permanently employed.

Similarly, in medicine, GPs have been accustomed to a mixed payment as independent contractors, receiving a fixed payment for each patient on the list and some variable amounts for an additional fee-for-item service.

Budgeting money

Working from the point of view that most doctors will be receiving a regular income in the form of a salary, you should consider the advice that Mr Micawber gives David Copperfield in Charles Dickens' classic novel:

> *'My other piece of advice, Copperfield,' said Mr Micawber, 'you know. Annual income twenty pounds, annual expenditure nineteen nineteen and six, result happiness. Annual income twenty pounds, annual expenditure twenty pounds ought and six, result misery. The blossom is blighted, the leaf is withered, the god of day goes down upon the dreary scene, and – and in short you are for ever floored. As I am!'*

Charles Dickens, *David Copperfield*, chapter 12

You can dress it up how you like ('Live now, pay later' – you will!) but this prosaic fact is relevant not only to your patients who don't know how to budget (apparently), but also to their doctors.

The problem is that you are almost certainly going to have less income than outgoings if you want to have a decent standard of living — at least in the early years of your professional life — and particularly when you decide that you want to own some property (though the Government may have helped you gain some experience of poverty and debt from the fees charged during your years as a medical student).

Some people have twigged the fact that if they run up large debts and then go bankrupt for a bit, they can, in effect, get what they want and have their creditors pay for it when the debts get cancelled. But this is not a decent way to behave, and it is damaging for the rest of society. And I am led to believe it is not too much fun for the person who has been bankrupted — with no access to such things as credit cards.

Let's assume that you don't want to behave like a crook (most people don't) and that you don't have a sugar daddy to bankroll you, then you have to look at what you are earning and what your expenditure is. It may be a boring thing to have to do sometime in the course of the working week, because when you get home, all you want to do is relax. But there are some habits that are worthwhile.

The banking system, for all its faults, allows people a great deal of control in terms of what they are doing with their money. For one thing, salaries can be paid to you directly. If you are an employee, you will have your pay, with tax already deducted, paid into your bank account. No-one can come up to you on pay day and steal the contents of your pay packet.

You also have a clear record of how much is coming in each month. You can use the banking system to ensure that your regular expenses (rent or mortgage payments, gas, electricity, water, telephone bills) are paid in a regular and timely fashion, by the use of standing orders and direct debits.

You can manage incidental expenditure by using a cheque book or credit or debit card. If you are going to do this, you must keep track of what you are spending. It is dull and time-consuming, but you must keep all dockets and stubs and compare them with the monthly credit-card bills. And you would be wise to limit the number of cards that you have. It is hard to keep track of more than two cards (one for personal use, one for business – if relevant). Do not be enticed into having loads of store cards. Again, it is easy to sign up, easy to get confused about what you owe — and easy to find yourself in piles of debt. Even the use of cash can be monitored, because, even if you do not track where you spend every last penny of cash, you can still get a good idea of how much cash you are using. So, it's quite simple really. Just work out if you are earning more than you spend — or spending more than you earn.

And so we come again to our favourite hobby horse in this chapter — choice. By having information about your use of money, you can decide which option you wish to take. It is not a moral issue (though people will talk to you as though it is). You can keep within your income — but that might mean limiting the number of times you can go to the cinema; or you can have a better time and allow yourself to go into debt, with the risk (but not the guarantee) of setting up a very nasty time for yourself some way down the line. Bank managers (unlike doctors) are not known for being full of the milk of human kindness, especially when they are owed significant sums of money. But do not ignore the fact either that many people who work in banks will work very hard to help you out of a tough spot — if you ask in the right way. The bottom line with your budget is that the choice is yours; and remember that there are times when you have to choose between two options, neither of which is satisfactory. This is one such choice.

The option of burying your head in the sand and pretending there is no problem with money (the 'ostrich syndrome') does not exist. Not that people don't ignore bills — they do. But to ignore debt and go on spending is actually making a positive choice to be in greater and greater debt. And burying your head in the sand — or 'denial', as we shrinks like to call it — only makes it harder for you to resolve the difficulties when the going gets tough. (As a side comment, and as this is a book for psychiatrists — antidepressants do not cure debt-induced misery). So, keep an eye on your finances. If you are going up a career ladder, your income should gradually increase, while your expenditure should not increase so quickly (until the children start to come along).

But, in the short term, what can you do if your sums don't balance? If your expenditure exceeds your income, you have two basic approaches:

- increase your income
- reduce your spending.

If you want to take the first approach — increase your income — you are going to have to do some additional work. It would mean giving up even more of that precious and limited time that you have for yourself. And it is further complicated by the fact that doctors are now being included in the European Working Time Directive, which limits the number of hours we are being permitted to work. The opportunity to do locum work is now quite limited.

You must also bear in mind that if you do additional work, you must still ensure that you are adequately rested and fit to do your main job. So finding things to do to earn serious amounts of extra money is not easy. The one thing that is particularly unhelpful is to take on additional work at a low hourly rate. If you want to increase your income significantly, you must value your time properly.

The second approach — reduce your spending — is also hard to achieve. Certain costs will be fairly fixed and may take up a significant portion of your budget. They may include your mortgage payments, utility bills and running a car — things that require expenditure. However, you should look at your other spending. There may be things that you can cut out. A common example is the purchase of goods where the price is increased. For example, if you buy a roll or lunch in the work canteen, you can be certain that you will be paying more than if you had bought the ingredients yourself. And the costs may add up quite quickly. And then there is the cost of all those beers and clothes. This part of your life may seem particularly difficult, but it is worth bearing in mind that, if you stay in roughly the same job situation over time, the financial situation will slowly improve.

Getting accommodation

Accommodation in some parts of the UK is affordable. In other parts, especially the south east, it is extremely expensive. For some workers, there is no other option but to stay with parents. You should think carefully about where (geographically) you want to live. It will, of course, depend on your preferred lifestyle. This decision will in turn affect where you apply for work.

There has been a tendency, as a result of improvements in transport, for people to live increasing distances from their place of work, and also from their closest. The effect of increased mobility has been to break up communities. Many people, therefore, find themselves cut off from their networks of support. It is wise to include a proper evaluation of the social network you want and will get from where you live and work.

If you are intending to have a solitary lifestyle, then it may not matter so much where you live. For people with elderly parents and young children, on the other hand, proximity to these relatives may be particularly worth considering.

Renting

In England there is a tradition of buying one's own home, if possible. In some countries in Europe, renting is more common. If you rent a property, either from the council or from a private landlord, it is 'dead money'. In other words, it does not matter how long you rent it for, and how much money you have paid in total, the property will never be yours.

However, if you rent the property, you will not be responsible for its maintenance. If it needs a new coat of paint or there is an electrical fault, you do not usually have to pay for it (unless it is specified in the rental agreement). There are therefore advantages and disadvantages in renting. You have greater flexibility and you do not have to find money to meet a mortgage. If your job involves frequent moves, then it is sometimes easier not to own the property.

If you do rent, you should obtain a contract from the landlord. A good landlord will use a standard contract, obtainable pre-printed from many good stationers. Having such a contract will reduce the extent of misunderstandings. As well as using your local Citizens' Advice Bureaux, you can also get information about renting, and about tenants' rights, from a variety of organisations (including the Consumers' Association, the publishers of the *Which?* series of magazines) and from the internet.

If you decide to share the flat or house with other people, especially if they are not your partner or family, you should be clear at the start who will hold the tenancy and who will be responsible for which tasks. You should draw up a clear agreement between you all, preferably with legal advice. It is better to make a clear binding agreement with friends you are sharing with and then find out you do not need it because you get on so well than to presume that you are such good friends that an agreement is unnecessary — only to have a row and great difficulty sorting it out.

Buying a property

Many people feel that it is in their interest to buy their property, if they can. The first step to take is to approach an estate agent. However obvious this may seem, what is less clear to someone coming from healthcare is that they are entering an alien world. The job of an estate agent is to sell houses. It is usually done on a commission basis, often a percentage of the sale. This means that if there is no sale, the agent gets no pay. Therefore, there is pressure on the agent to persuade people to buy. In an ideal sale, there should be a willing seller and a willing buyer with a price that both are happy with. This does occur, and reputable agents will try to achieve it. But you should be aware that some agents will be under pressure to get a sale agreed, even if the parties are not entirely happy with it. The agent may use a number of devices to persuade you — ensure that you get the house that you want and can afford. If you are not happy, then say no. Your job is to get the right house for you, not to please a salesman.

You should start by getting an idea of how much you can afford. As a rule of thumb, if you are buying on your own, you can afford a mortgage of two and a half times your annual salary. If you are buying with a spouse or partner, you can afford a mortgage of a total of two and a half times the larger salary and one and a half times the smaller salary. Estate agents and financial advisers may glibly tell you that you can afford more than this. However, the reason for these multiples is that they are also a guide to the costs of running the house. The greater the cost of purchase, the greater the running costs, including council charge. There is no point owning a house if you cannot afford to turn on the heating or cook your supper.

A particular issue arises if you are buying with your spouse and you plan to have children. Although many women insist that they will return to work (or insist that both partners will work) after the baby is born, the arrival of the newcomer often changes attitudes. Or, sometimes, the cost of the childminder is the equivalent of one whole salary. If you base a mortgage on both partners working, it puts a serious strain on the family finances if one partner then stops working to look after the child or children. While you will naturally be keen to get the best house you can when you buy, it will create serious problems if you cannot maintain mortgage repayments.

Unless you have the funds to buy the property outright, you are likely to need a large loan to pay for the house. The loan will be secured on the property. In other words, the bank or building society who agree to loan you the money will require that you give the building as security – if you do not keep up repayments on the loan, they can sell the property against your will to recover the money you owe them.

You should look around at the various offers available from different companies. At the time of writing, interest rates are particularly low, but you should be wary of how affordable this makes your purchase. You may prefer to take a fixed-interest loan, but if the loan is of variable interest rate (even after a period of fixed rate), then what was a manageable at 6% at the time of purchase becomes an entirely unmanageable amount if interest rates go up to 12%. You need to understand the different types of mortgage (repayment, endowment, etc) and what they mean for you. Look carefully for independent advice through consumer-rights groups.

The mortgage company will insist that you have the house examined by a qualified person, usually a chartered surveyor, to confirm that the house is in good order and not just about to fall down. Even if they do not, you should arrange such a survey to reassure yourself of the house's safety and stability. The estate agent or the building society may be able to recommend a surveyor. You should try to arrange a fixed fee for the survey.

Having found a mortgage company willing to lend you the money you need, in a form that you can afford, they will then make a mortgage offer. Mortgage companies will often try to sell you financial products (eg. critical illness cover for mortgage-repayment protection, house and content insurance). Remember that this is about selling, not about concern for your welfare. Some companies are tied, and are limited in the financial products they can sell. Others are driven by commission rates. They may try to sell you what is best for them rather than for you. They may not. Just be cautious.

Having decided that you like a property, you then make an offer. In England, you are not committed to the purchase at that stage. If the vendor (seller) accepts your offer, you need to give the estate agent the name of your solicitor. If you do not have a solicitor, the estate agent may be able to recommend one. There are also conveyancers (the legal process of buying a house is called a conveyance) who are not legally qualified, but who are able to process straightforward transactions. They should have connections with a solicitor.

When you contact the solicitor, you should ask for a clear statement of how much you will be charged for the whole process (including VAT). Ideally, the solicitor should give you a fixed fee, variable only if the transaction turns out to be unusually complicated. You should also ask how much additional payments you have to make. The additional costs include a local authority search to ensure that there are no public plans that would make purchasing the house unwise (eg. you purchase a property for £160,000 when the council have already published that they plan to demolish the house to make way for a new road); a search of the Land Registry for proof of title (in other words, does the State recognise that the person selling the house actually owns it?); the stamp duty (which can be a significant amount, in thousands of pounds); and various disbursements (small amounts for photocopying and postage, for instance). You will need to have all this money available at the time of purchase.

The vendor's solicitor will prepare a contract and send it to your solicitor. Your solicitor will prepare a set of additional enquiries about what is included in the sale (the curtains? the light bulbs?) and the state of the house (any problems with neighbours, the drains, etc). You should read all documents carefully and, if you do not understand anything, you should ask your solicitor. Do not sign anything until you are completely satisfied.

And do not let yourself off with, 'I'm too busy to read all that stuff'. Of course, you are a busy doctor and finding time is not easy. But if you sign something, you are committed to it. Saying that you were too busy to read it doesn't get your money back — and, in the case of a property, we are talking a great deal of money. Set some time aside to read the various documents thoroughly, even if it means giving up something pleasurable.

When both sides are happy with the contractual arrangements, the solicitors will invite both parties to exchange contracts. Be aware that it can take a matter of weeks from giving the offer to exchange of contracts. You may be asked to make a deposit of 5–10% of the purchase price at the time of exchange.

Once you have exchanged contracts, you are committed to the purchase. It may take a few more days before you are in a position to hand over the money. Your solicitor will receive the money from the mortgage company and will hold it on your behalf. Only when the money is handed over does the property become yours. This is called completion, and it is then that you can move in.

Sometimes, the vendor is buying a new property and is timing it to coincide with the sale of the property you are buying. Completion of these two purchases will therefore be occurring on the same day. And the vendor's vendor may be doing the same. When several purchases are taking place at one time, it is referred to as a 'chain'. If one cannot complete, the whole chain breaks down, making it a problem for everyone.

After you have purchased the property, you are responsible for it entirely. If the loo breaks, it is up to you to fix it. If the carpet drives you nuts, it is up to you to find the money to replace it or learn to live with it. You will want to insure the building against various risks, such as subsidence or any other reason for it cracking up. You will also have to pay the Council Tax, the water rates, gas, electricity, TV licence. Before you buy, you can ask the vendor for copies of recent bills. It will help you to plan for these costs.

If you have budgeted for all these things, living in a house becomes much more manageable. There will be additional costs (telephone, gardening [if there is one], service charge in blocks of flats, plumbing, electrical emergencies, redecoration) that you should anticipate. You have to think about all of this in your spare time.

Getting married

A party game for you to play. Next time you are out at a gathering – dinner party, political gathering, conference, or just the cafeteria – listen out for how many people say:

⌘ 'We're living together, but we're not going to get married. After all, it's only a piece of paper.'
⌘ 'Now that I am with John/Jane, I'm not going to change. I'm still the person I was before I was with him/her.'

Now, whatever my personal ethical beliefs, this part of the book is not an essay on morals. But as a psychiatrist (you, as well as me), it is striking how dismissive people are about a major life change. I don't mean moving from being single to being married — but moving from being single to entering a phase of life in which you are one of two (legally married or not), with a view perhaps to being one of three, six, ten or however many you end up with. The point is that, in becoming a proper couple, you are creating a new social unit. I don't mean to be rude about people who produce the types of statement I have just mentioned. But I do think such statements require a bit more thought.

Imagine that someone owed you a large amount of money. They wrote you a cheque, but did not sign it. You take the cheque and go to the bank. They won't cash it for you. You argue, you plead. 'But it's not signed,' the bank clerk says, 'the person has not indicated that they want us to hand the money over, so there's nothing I can do to help you.'

Your initial reaction might be that there was no problem. You would say to yourself that you will just go back to the person, ask them to sign, then present the cheque to the bank again. On many occasions, when it was a genuine mistake on the part of an honest person, that goes without a hitch. But what if the person who owes you money goes bankrupt after they give you the cheque? They may have had money in the bank at the original time that they gave you the cheque, but don't have any more. Or what if you don't know their address? Or what if they live too far away for you to find them and get them to sign it? Or what if the cheque gets lost in the post. What if they simply tell you to get stuffed? Wouldn't it have been simpler just to have got it signed in the first place?

Getting married involves signing on the dotted line. Once you have done so, the law treats you and your spouse differently to when you were single, even if you were living together. It doesn't matter if you got married in Westminster Abbey or Westminster Registry Office, the law treats all people who have got married the same — and it distinguishes the married from the unmarried.

'But,' I hear our cohabitees reply, 'we've been living together for twenty years. Surely that makes us entitled to the same benefits as married people?' The Law descends from On High: 'But only married people are entitled to have the benefits of marriage. How am I to know that you are married, if you refuse to tell me? I only know that people are married when they tell me by getting legally married.'

If you want the law to think you're married, sign on the dotted line. If you don't, don't be surprised if the law doesn't pay up when your partner goes and dies on you.

Now, I really don't care how you choose to live your life – single, celibate, serially monogamous, bigamous, gay, hetero, intersex, in a harem, in a commune, with a herd of yaks. It's your choice. As long as you're happy, that's fine by me. In fact, it's really none of my business.

But what is curious to us as psychiatrists is that there is a great deal of evidence that people who live together without getting married do not have the same level of commitment to the relationship as people who do. I know there will be individual examples to the contrary — there are plenty of straying spouses and faithful cohabitees. It's just that the frequent observation that separation is more common among cohabitees than among married people suggests that a cohabitee is likely to be less committed to the relationship (and more accepting of the notion of a split) than is a married person. By all means, live with someone, and go round saying, 'it's only a piece of paper,' but in your heart of hearts, know that it is not. Choices are always better when you make them with your eyes open.

What about the second statement that now that you are living with someone or married to them, you are the same person you were? Well, biologically, you are. But socially, psychologically and emotionally, you are not. Once you have started a serious relationship with someone, you have responsibilities to that person.

Responsibilities are the hallmark of growing up. You may not like it. When you accept responsibilities, you may envy those without them. James Bond films (and books) are fantasies in which the central character is suave, clever and good-looking. He drinks alcohol ('Vodka Martini — shaken, not stirred') without becoming drunk. He shoots other people without being injured. He has unprotected intercourse without having babies (or at least not taking responsibility for them) and without getting a sexually transmitted disease. He is up at all hours of the day, for days on end, without getting tired.

But he does not exist. Whichever way the media try to present some remarkable individuals in society, they just do not have James Bond's capabilities. Why else are our top celebrities in and out of alcohol and drug rehab?

In the week after you have come back from your honeymoon, you may go out with the lads/girls for a jar on Thursday night, just as you did the week before you got married. But it is not the same, because there is now someone you have to account to when you get back.

You may wonder, therefore, why people bother to get married and to take on responsibilities. But let's take an example to consider one of many different scenarios. You don't want to take responsibility. So you go off and father a child (unplanned or not) and leave the mother to get on with it, or decide that you are not bothered about getting pregnant, but you have no intention of looking after it when it's born. Many years later, you are talking to the grown-up child you didn't bother with and you can't understand why they don't care about you.

What we are talking about in this section is a major life change. I repeat — whether, when and how you choose to do it is up to you. But the problem with such changes is that you don't usually understand them until you have been through them. You need the information to get through them while you are going through them, not before. When you find yourself in a marital spot of bother, you look back and think, 'How did this all happen?' You can bury your head in the sand and go down the pub. Or you can think what did happen, and notice how you have changed.

Being married (or truly committed to someone else, in a heterosexual or homosexual relationship) is quite different from being single. It is not just that you are two people rather than one, but that you are a new unit. Let me offer another example. It is a hot summer's night. You and your partner went out for the evening, and when you returned, you put your wallets on the kitchen table when you had a drink there. You then went to bed, forgetting to move your wallets. As (bad) luck would have it, you also forgot to close the window. Later that night, a burglar sees the open window and climbs in. He sees the two wallets on the table. They are clearly identified, one belonging to you and the other to your partner. Does the burglar think, 'Well, I must find out which one of them left the window open and only take that person's wallet?' Or does he take them both?

The point is that when people are living as a unit, whoever makes the mistake, you all suffer. It is, of course, the exact opposite of the phenomenon that if one of you does something well, you all gain. The most simple example is (in the old-fashioned way) when the man went out to work and brought home his wages, the money psychologically belongs to the unit (husband and wife, plus or minus children and any other relatives or assorted hangers-on). This way of thinking is crucial to the functioning of the unit because it means that you are responsible for your partner's mistakes (and vice versa). If your partner, or you, spends money on a new car, then you both have less money to go on holiday. And it's no good going to the bank manager and asking him to restore your bank balance because your partner spent your joint money in a way that you are not happy with — any more than you will get anywhere ringing up the person who burgled your house (if you knew where to find him) and asking him to return your wallet, but not your partner's as it was your partner that left the window open.

The importance of recognising that you are jointly responsible for each other's decisions is that, when things get tough, you can go one of two ways. Either you can become hyper-critical of each other and hate each other — with the risk that you will start to make additional mistakes as you try and score points off each other — or you can recognise that you each have the right to make mistakes, but that it helps if you talk about them. Such conversations indicate trust and respect, the very commodities that are at the heart of a good marriage and which make marriage such a strong institution. Problems are automatically shared and the future can be planned together.

Being jointly responsible is also an indication of the fact that being married is a peer relationship. In other words, neither of you is the parent and neither of you is the child. I know that if you have read Eric Berne's *Games People Play*, you will read that people adopt 'parent', 'adult' and 'child' positions in relation to each other. I am not disagreeing with this analysis of interpersonal interactions; but I am talking at a much more superficial level. When you were a child, if something went wrong, it was up to your mother or father to help you. They supported you, emotionally and physically, and they did the work. You might have been vaguely aware that they were tired, but, ultimately, you felt that it was up to them to help you. They were responsible for washing, cooking, getting you to places on time, and consoling you when something upset you.

Whatever type of person you have chosen as your spouse, even if you have looked for a father or a mother figure, it is up to you to provide the support for them as much as to expect support from them. You are not more important, nor are you less. Of course, there are spouses who do all the supportive tasks their other half needs, and if you have a spouse who does everything you want, then you are fortunate. More likely, when you come home tired at the end of a hard day, you will come home to a spouse who is also tired from a hard day (even if your spouse has been at home all day, it does not mean that he or she has not had a busy and exhausting time). You cannot assume that your drama needs listening to, while your spouse's does not (or vice versa). It isn't romantic, it isn't always easy, but if you can be aware of it, you will not have unrealistic expectations and a source of tension in your marriage will be significantly reduced.

There is one more point I want to make about marriage before we look at the issues of marriage as a doctor and, more particularly, as a psychiatrist. In the selection of long-term partners, we subconsciously choose people with a lot of similarities to ourselves. So, when you look at the things that irritate you most about your partner, you can be pretty sure that they are faults that you have. Have a look in the mirror before you have a go at your partner.

What are the issues for doctors when they are spouses? Medicine has always been a demanding profession. Despite major shifts (in public, at any rate) by the managerial powers, it is still the case that many doctors work long weeks. As with all other resources, working long hours means that there are less hours available to be spent with the family. The impact of the long hours may not be understood or acknowledged by the spouse. In one poignant (and, hopefully, extreme) example, a junior paediatrician who had been on-call and working the previous night was expected by his wife (a nurse) to go to a party when he came home. Also, the structure of the junior years has for a long time been based on changes of job — and with it, sometimes, changes of accommodation — every six months. Spouses of doctors may not be happy with the constant shifting and lack of stability, but, in the present climate, when doctors no longer take a position for life, the instability can continue for much longer than it did previously.

The situation is not helped by the fact that doctors are less well-paid than they used to be. It is important to bear in mind that doctors are still paid significantly more than average, but the pressure on doctors (as on other groups in society) is that it is increasingly hard to obtain a good standard of living on one salary alone.

This raises the question of whether both spouses should work, especially if both are medically qualified. So, let us start by dealing with the issue of 'equality' in wages. It is a misrepresentation of feminism to suggest that there is a viewpoint that both partners in a relationship should work and that there is no reason why a woman should not earn her own money. In a properly working family, the money should not belong to the earner (any more than the clean knife, fork and dish should only be used by the person who washed it). It should be 'common property'. As such, the spouses should devise mechanisms to permit equal access (eg. a joint bank account). Of course, it does not matter which partner brings in the money — and the decision should not be based on the shape of the genitals. What is important is that the couple work out what is the most effective for them.

This does not mean that, for a couple who decide that they will both work, they should not do so. What it does mean is that they must sort out between them who will do the other marital tasks — such as the cooking, shopping, cleaning and paying the bills. Often, there is no discussion and one of the partners ends up doing it by default. There are some couples for whom this arrangement works; but for those for whom it does not, you need to stand back and use some of the little time available to you as a couple to clarify the situation.

Perhaps one of the most difficult questions of working in a caring profession might be (to paraphrase the Roman poet Juvenal), 'Who will care for the carers?' If you are a doctor and you work hard to care for your patients — and psychiatry is especially demanding, emotionally — then when you get home at the end of a long day, you will want some time and space for yourself. Preferably with someone to mop your fevered brow.

But one of your attractions to your partner is that you are a caring person. Your partner may expect you to care for his or her needs. And for a psychiatrist, your partner may have chosen you (subconsciously or otherwise) for your listening skills, even though you are too tired to deploy them at the end of a hard working day. There is no 'correct' resolution to this. Your partner does have a right to your time and your attention and you have a right to switch off. The potential for conflict is obvious. As with all pitfalls, you should know about them and address them. In this case, address them together.

Having a doctor in the family presents a relative with an ideal opportunity to avoid going to the GP. If you are that doctor in the family, you need to take a big breath and get ready to say 'no'. There is a saying that a doctor who treats himself has a fool for a patient. A relative who asks for treatment has a fool for a doctor. The problem is that if you try to treat a relative, you invariably distort your clinical perspective. And it is very easy to venture into areas of medicine in which you have little or no expertise. For your relative, perhaps the insignificant lump might be cancer. You might err on the side of prescribing an antibiotic that you would not consider for an unrelated patient, and increase your relative's exposure to immunogenicity. Your relative might bully you into prescribing an addictive drug such as a benzodiazepine hypnotic that you don't really want to prescribe. It is very difficult to be sure that you would treat such a relative exactly as you would treat a patient in your surgery. And the General Medical Council would disapprove, even if you were not actually struck off.

Don't treat relatives. It will be your (non-medical) spouse who puts the greatest pressure on you to do so. Make it clear that the relative should seek an independent medical opinion — his or her own GP or, in an emergency, the hospital's accident and emergency (A&E) department. If someone asks you if it wouldn't be easier to save everyone the hassle, just tell them that if getting proper medical advice is a hassle, then it shows that no medical advice is needed. Get this message across early and regularly — firmly, but politely.

The only exceptions are life-threatening emergencies for which an ambulance could not arrive in time, for example, cardiac arrest (basic CPR, not advanced), asthma, hypoglycaemia, anaphylaxis. Though note that an independent doctor would advise any family member to treat these — which doctor would not ask a non-medical mother to bring a ventilator of salbutamol when the child has an attack? In most cases, you are still acting as a lay person, not as a doctor. And once the immediate life-threatening phase is over, hand over to independent professionals.

As modern society considers the issue of work-life balance, certain questions will come more into focus. Of course, you should do your job appropriately and as thoroughly as you can in the time available. And, of course, you should not pander to every demand of your spouse. But when you are considering a decision between your work's interests and your spouse's, you should always put your spouse first.

This section on marriage may have come across as disorganised and idiosyncratic. In some ways, it is. You can find the basics of a good marriage widely available in the popular press — choose someone you like; treat them with respect, not contempt (ie. don't take them for granted); listen to what they say they want, not what you think is good for them; make time for them. And these are important principles. What I have tried to do is help you understand some of the dilemmas of the working person regarding their primary relationship — that with their partner or spouse.

Having children

Odd though it may seem, this is another of those major life changes. Once the little bundle of joy has come along — or even once it has been confirmed in the uterus — life is never the same again.

Suddenly, all the things that seemed boring and mundane become crucial and overwhelming. The wild, carefree life (or so it will seem) that you had before there were three of you feels an aeon ago. And all those trendies are looking down on you with pity.

Well — get real, everyone. Children are the future of our species. They are also the ones who will push you around in your wheelchair. It is their work that will pay your pension. If you decided you were a 'free spirit' in your youth and that nappies (diapers) were for fools, then what right have you to expect that you will be looked after in your dotage?

For those of you who think there is a bias here, be aware that you have the right to choose. Of course, you have the right not to have children — and many do not. Some, on the other hand, are childless against their will. The point (again) is that all choices have consequences.

But do not underestimate the new world you will be entering when your first child is born. As with any other life event, people will look at you in a different way afterwards, so you had better get ready for it. Once you have got a child, your priorities change. You can still go drinking with the boys and/or girls, but you will be ignoring your duties. Between you, your other half, and any other person you can get to look after the little darling.

I am not saying that you will not need breaks – you will. But more of that later. (Did you consider your social network when you got your job and your place to live?) But those parents who are around for their kids see their friends only sporadically, late at night or with bleary eyes. There are long periods when you just can't keep in touch. But you have got a bundle of joy: a demanding, selfish, overwhelming bundle of joy.

Another of those choices. Demanding, selfish or joyful? The answer depends on what you want. What I am about to say, albeit perhaps in a somewhat loose style, is echoed by other people's experiences (see *Table 3.1*) and backed up by a great deal of research.

The bottom line is that you have to treat your child (as you should your wife, parents, siblings and in-laws) with courtesy and respect. And lots of love. This is not a matter of gooey-sicky-loveliness; it is a matter of whether you want a well-adjusted happy child or an angry, hostile, sullen, drug-using anti-social potential crook (or someone pretty much on the way to being one). A bit black and white, you might say — and forgive me for a bit of dramatic exaggeration — but the evidence is quite clear. Care properly for your child and you will make a big difference.

Courtesy, respect and love, you say? Does this mean that you have to give in to every little whim? Of course not. Respecting somebody involves accepting them as a person in their own right, with their own wants, likes and needs — while at the same time expecting them to respect others (in accordance with their age and ability). So, if you are on the phone talking to a friend, you can tell your young toddler to wait for a minute for whatever he or she is asking for. But make sure that you do stop soon and pay attention to what your toddler wants — it may not be appropriate to continue talking to your friend for another hour (unless it is something highly important and urgent). It is this give-and-take that shows that you are concerned for your child, but expect him or her to consider (in a more limited way) your needs too.

An important example is bed time — many children do not want to let their parents go. But (especially when your child is young), when you put them to bed, you do not have to stay with them until they fall asleep. It is perfectly reasonable for you to limit the time you spend (even to a very few minutes). Many people feel guilty in response to their child begging them not to go. You should say how long you will stay (eg. five minutes) and then stick rigidly to it. You should also explain to your child that, while you realise that you must spend time with him or her, you also need some time for yourself. It is not a matter of selfishness, but teaching the child that his or her parent also has needs to which they are entitled. If you say this firmly (but not angrily), and caringly, the child will not object. If you do it every day, the child will get used to it and accept it without demur. And you will both be happier.

Table 3.1: The ten golden rules of parenting

1. Love infuses all parenting principles.

2. Every child needs respect.

3. Every child needs to be listened to.

4. Parents should attempt to understand their children and respond appropriately.

5. Good parenting gives boundaries and limits by using alternatives to physical violence.

6. Children learn by example, so act as you want your child to act.

7. There is no such thing as a perfect parent; involve others or get support.

8. Have fun with your children.

9. Be willing to learn from your children.

10. Be realistic about the world, but give your children the self-confidence to know that they can make a difference.

The Times, 'Global Family Therapy' 15 September, 2003

Perhaps the most helpful comment I ever saw was the title of Bruno Bettleheim's book *A Good Enough Parent*. It isn't a competition. There are no grades. You don't have to be perfect — just good enough. You are entitled to have headaches and be tired and not want to come and play all the time. But if you snap at your child because you have a headache, tell the child that you are sorry for snapping and that it is not his or her fault.

If you let your child grow up feeling his or her needs are considered, but respecting that he or she has to do things and that there are limits to freedom ('No, darling, you can't have a third chocolate biscuit.' 'Why not, mummy?' 'Because two is enough.' 'Why?' 'Because two is enough.' — all said calmly and politely), discipline is much less of a problem. The issue of smacking is much less relevant. Smiles, hugs and kisses, all done appropriately, also help the child feel the world is a supportive place.

Tantrums do occur in the best of children. They are a non-verbal way of showing distress. The problem is that if the child goes into a tantrum, he or she cannot be talked out of it. It is no good getting angry with the child and telling it to stop — the child cannot stop even if it wants to. The best way to handle a tantrum is to hold the child in your arms. Keep holding the child until the thrashing around subsides. It does, and the child nestles into your arms, calms down, and feels warm towards you. You have contained your child's distress. Over time, it will learn from you that it can contain its own distress. But it needed your lesson and support.

Enough of the pop parent guide. You can get much more information from other parents (including your own!) and the excellent guides that are available (those by Penelope Leach and Steve Biddulph are good examples [*Chapter 6*]). And don't fall into the trap of thinking that, because you are a doctor, you know how to handle children. If you have done several years as a junior paediatrician; are highly competent at handling difficult behaviour in patients and staff (especially manipulation); and are a consultant in child psychiatry — then just maybe you have covered most of it (in which case, don't forget to include the bits about what to do as a significantly older parent). Otherwise, you would be wise to recall that a little knowledge can be a dangerous thing.

You will find, even as a medically qualified parent, that there are a whole host of situations that you come across that, if you are honest with yourself, you do not have a clue about. And when you do find out about them, you learn that they are common. If you have a problem, do not get on your high horse ('I am a doctor. I don't need anyone to tell me anything'). Ask whoever is around: your mother; your brother or sister; your friend; the other parents at school; the old lady down the road; the pharmacist; indeed, anyone who has had a child. And ask **several** people — you will occasionally get different answers, but you'll learn from that too. And don't fear ridicule. It is not a crime not to know something; no question is too stupid to ask. And you will probably find that they are only too happy to advise, often with a great deal of good sense.

If your child is not well, do not even consider treating him or her yourself. Just as when you were a medical student, you thought that the most innocent symptoms meant you had a terminal illness, so, as a parent, you need to be aware that you know both too much and too little. Of course, a sniffle could be an early sign of something like leukaemia, but you will remember another maxim that you heard repeated *ad nauseam* in medical school — that common things are common. So that sniffle is most likely to be a cold. If you are worried, ask your GP. When you go, help by giving a clear history, but other than that remember that you are no more than an educated parent. Listen to the advice you are given — don't allow yourself to tell the GP what to do.

Fitting parenting in with work is a major headache — both for you and for all the patients who come saying that they can't cope with a full-time job and looking after their children. Hopefully, you will not have had an attitude before having children that you realise you need to change after becoming a parent yourself.

The fact is that being a parent is a full-time job. And bringing up the next generation is the most important job in the world. There is no occupation that is more important — everything else merely supports that basic truth. You may be a doctor or a computer whizzkid or a City financier, but all these jobs provide support for the most important task. Making money is only one aspect of life, not the whole. For an extreme example, but to make the point, look at the life of J Paul Getty. A highly successful oilman, he made vast amounts of money. But his neglect — indeed, abuse of his family — meant that his money did nothing. His children had a whole range of problems, one dying from a heroin overdose. Just because being a parent is not a paid job, don't underestimate its value. Ideally, one parent (of either sex) should be at home to bring up the child.

Of course, while money isn't everything, you can't do entirely without it. So, it may be that both parents have to work. If so, there is no need to feel guilty about having to go to work if your circumstances mean you do not have a choice (or if you are simply happier working than parenting). But make proper arrangements.

For all its bureaucracy, the Western world (especially Europe) is really starting to recognise the importance of making allowance for its workers to be parents as well. In the NHS, you have a range of entitlements as a parent. For the mother, there is maternity leave, including the right to stay at home for one year (though not all of it is paid) and then expect your old job back. For men, there is also support. They are likely to be supported going to antenatal clinics. They can have paternity leave when the child is born, and parental leave (a number of days taken off within the first five years of life). There is also exceptional leave granted for times when necessary, such as if your child is ill and off school one day. And this is all in addition to standard leave (annual leave, sick leave, etc). You will need to check the details of the available entitlements and ensure that you take them. (With several European directives, the entitlements are undergoing much change — you will need to find out the current allowances. Human resource officers can often help.)

In a well-run unit, these entitlements simply provide a formal backup to the normal give-and-take in any work environment. If the team is functioning properly, this is part of the routine give and take. If you are asking a colleague to cover some of your work while you take leave, it is prudent to help them out when he or she needs it, if you can. In a poorly managed unit, you may have to assert your rights. If you do take your entitlement, it is up to the manager – not you – to ensure that you are covered in your absence. You must of course give adequate notice when you can and assist the manager in working out how your work can be covered in your absence.

Workers without children may complain that your taking your leave entitlement because of your children puts them at an unfair disadvantage. They might feel that they have to do a greater share of the work because you are taking your leave. This needs to be handled delicately, and where possible, a good manager will try to ensure that the imbalance in the distribution of work is as small as possible. But it should not make you lose your entitlements.

You may also have to review what you do in your job a little more closely. You will be under greater pressure to leave on time, to get back to your children and you may not be able to see the extra patient in the clinic. You may need to decline additional commitments a bit earlier. You may also need to be sure about the back-up plans for looking after your kids when you are unavoidably detained by a patient's urgent medical needs.

There is a lot of information available about different working arrangements to facilitate looking after children. You may work on a part-time or sessional basis. Your job may permit you to do some work at home, though this is less likely in the junior stages of working as a doctor.

Divorce

Divorce is never pleasant at the best of times. But for a psychiatrist (or psychotherapist), there is the added sense of shame that, as an expert in relationships, your marriage should not fail. You should have known better.

Actually, you shouldn't. The chances are that you went into a psychological branch of psychiatry because, at some level, you have an interest in relationships. So, for you, relationships are a learning process, both individually and observationally with your patients.

It is well to remember that divorces don't happen over night. Problems in a relationship have often been evident for some time, but part of you found it difficult to acknowledge what was going on. You may also have embarked on the relationship from which you are about to split before you had your training.

Having realised what is going on — that your relationship is at an end — you will need practical, legal and emotional advice. The way help is organised means that you may not be able to get all the advice you need from only one person, source or organisation. You will almost certainly have to go to a family lawyer for legal advice and to some sort of marriage guidance counsellor to look at the emotional aspects. As a start to the legal process, you may wish to consult a guide such as the *Which? Guide to Divorce*, but there are other manuals. You should consult friends for the name of a good family lawyer who deals with divorces.

As for the emotional aspects, you can start with your doctor (GP), who may (or may not) have sufficient interest in people and sufficient experience of life (and other patients who have experienced relationship difficulties) to be able to help in a general way. Or you may seek organisations that deal with relationships, such as Relate.

This book will focus more on the emotional and practical issues, rather than the legal ones. But remember I am not offering advice, but guidance — a few initial thoughts that may form the basis for you to make more effective use of the services available.

Let us just think a little more about the different types of advice on offer — the legal and the emotional — because we can see the opportunity for a great deal of confusion. As things are at the moment, the legal system is, ultimately, adversarial. This means that in the courts of law, the two sides are fighting each other. The game is winner-takes-all, and the aim is to beat your opponent. Your lawyer, whose job is to get the very best that he or she can for you, will have to fight to get the other side to concede to you as much as possible. From the lawyer's point of view, the aim is to get everything — the children, the house, the car, the money in the bank accounts, all future earnings of your spouse, the pension, the dog, the little twiddly thing that goes 'whurr' and anything else — for you, and leave your soon-to-be-ex- with nothing. (And your partner's lawyer has the job of trying to do exactly the same to you.)

Now, in the heat of the crisis, as you and your spouse try to argue this through, it may seem a great idea to try and get everything you can. After all, you are angry. If you are the person leaving, you will feel that you are leaving for good reasons and your partner who has put you in this position doesn't deserve anything. If you are the person who has been deserted/left/cheated on, you may well feel that it is outrageous that such a cad should leave with anything. And the situation may be complicated by the fact that one of you may have started the tug of possessions by some action — such as clearing the house out or stopping payments on a credit card.

In contrast, the emotional services are trying to help the two of you work collaboratively. They can help you before the decision to split has been taken by offering the two of you a space to meet and talk about your differences. A good relationship counsellor will make it clear that it is not their role to adjudicate and will stop either of you trying to score points. The aim is that you should each have the opportunity to put into words things that you have thought but not said (or felt your partner had not heard), to look at whether there really is a difference.

For example, at one end of the spectrum, it may be that with both of you going out to work and trying to look after the kids, there is simply not enough time to be together. In such circumstances, you may both end up too tired to make love, or even to talk to each other. A marriage guidance counsellor might help you both to say that you do actually still love each other, but that you have both been too tired to say and do the things that show you care.

You may be able to agree that you need to make simple adjustments; for example, recognising that you would feel much more supported if you made a point of going out together once a week, or gave each other a kiss before going to sleep — things that you may have originally done without thinking at the beginning of your relationship, but which got lost in the demands of everyday adult life. Such simple things may rescue a marriage based on secure foundations that is wavering in the gale of outside demands.

At the other end of the spectrum, the discussion that the two of you have, facilitated by the counsellor, may make it clear that the overlap that brought you together no longer exists. Something has changed, or one of you has moved on — or maybe there was never a real basis for a close relationship at the start. In such circumstances, the discussion may help you both realise that the relationship is over and make the decision to separate.

Whatever the state of your relationship when you go to see the counsellor, the aim is to get the best outcome for the two of you. It is intended to be fair to both, not to pick out a winner.

To put it somewhat crudely, the approach of a lawyer is likely to be confrontational, whereas the approach of a counsellor is likely to be conciliatory. And the advice you receive from each may well be conflicting. (Although this distinction is not always so clear-cut. For example, the lawyer may insist that the two of you attempt some mediated settlement — one in which a mutually acceptable solution is drawn up first — before confronting each other. And poor counsellors may let their own opinions get in the way of your discussion.) However, you should be prepared for these two different types of advice as you might eventually have to choose between them.

Before you get to the stage of taking the decision to divorce, you will be thinking about the state of your relationship beforehand. At difficult times, especially when emotions are running high, it is easy to make snap decisions. As with any major life-decision, you should take your time and not do anything unless you are sure that you are happy to accept the consequences. In particular, you should remind yourself that trust is the basis of any relationship. You should not do anything that cannot be interpreted any other way than as a breach of trust before you are clear that you are going to separate.

So do not have sex outside marriage; do not send your partner a rude text message saying you are dumping him or her; do not transfer money from a joint account into a separate single account; do not obtain another place to live; and do not walk out of the door unless you mean to declare that the relationship is over. These issues are irreversible. Once you have been sexually unfaithful to your partner, even if you then agree to stay together, your sexual fidelity can never be taken for granted again. You cannot return to the role of the faithful spouse — because you are not. And, if you feel the need to have sex with someone other than your spouse, you should wait until you have made it clear to your spouse that the relationship is over.

Once the two of you have made the decision that divorce will go ahead, you may feel a range of unpleasant emotions; anger, shock, confusion, betrayal, hurt, hatred, physical nausea, guilt, and a fear of the future. You may feel like a second-class citizen and envy couples who are still together, with a sense that 'it's not fair'. Your mutual friends may start to take sides (some against you) and accusations and blame may begin.

At moments of high emotion, it is easy to make unwise decisions. When it comes to thinking about all the things you have to discuss (the house, the kids, the car), you must try to behave in a reasonable manner. You should look for a reasonable settlement — as will any judge, if the two of you decide to go at each other hammer and tongs. If you are vindictive, you are likely to end up with even less, for example, if you have lots of disputes through lawyers, you will both incur high legal costs, leaving less money to be divided between the two of you. In an acrimonious divorce, it is very easy to cut off your nose to spite your face.

Bear in mind, too, that two people who have divorced may see what happened in their marriage very differently. As a means of negotiating an amicable settlement, it is useful to gain some understanding of what your ex-spouse thinks happened between you. To understand someone else's point of view is not the same as accepting it as correct — but it does allow you the opportunity to avoid aggravating the situation.

People who have commented on divorce from experience or expertise point out that divorce is forever. What they mean is that you may well have to continue having contact with the person you have divorced. You may have to continue to make payments. You may have to meet each other on a regular basis as part of the custody arrangements, even if only when you go to leave or collect your children from each other. I am not going to comment here on the effect of divorce on your children — you should seek advice from the services mentioned earlier.

After the legal process of divorce is settled, you will still find that there is a process that you will go through as you come to terms with what has happened. You are now a single person again. You have had what you might see as a major life failure (whoever was at fault). You will have to take on tasks that your ex-spouse used to do for you — whether it is washing your own laundry or doing homework with your children. You will find that your married friends are not always in tune with you. They may try to get you paired off when you are not ready. Social engagements may become more trying. And when you are ready to find someone new, you may be much less confident.

But if you recognise that, once all the legal issues are dealt with, the marriage is over and you must move on, you can come to terms with it and reconstruct your life in a positive way.

Working with a disability

At the time of writing this book, the UK Home Secretary is blind. Whatever your political viewpoint, and however you regard him as doing the job, the fact is that one of the members of the Government is performing one of the senior jobs in Cabinet while living with a major disability. I am not going to patronise David Blunkett by admiring his achievement in the face of such an obstacle — he has plenty of people to do that for him. My point in raising the example of David Blunkett is that many jobs can be done in spite of disability. Someone like David Blunkett uses his highly able mind and political skills, experience and expertise — because these are the things that you need to do the job of Home Secretary, whether or not you can see. Any politician needs to be able to read documents and to interact with other people, especially recognising their non-verbal body language. Using the sense of sight is the easiest way of reading and communicating non-verbally. But there are other ways to do these things, and Mr Blunkett has found suitable alternatives, getting documents he needs to read translated into Braille, listening to the radio rather than watching television to get the news, and using his other senses to pick up a great deal of non-verbal information.

So the question is not, 'Should I stop myself applying for a job because of my disability?' or 'Should I leave this job now that I have developed a disability?', but rather, 'What knowledge/skills/abilities does the job I would like to do require, and do I have them?'

A disability is simply a recognition that there is something that a person with a disability cannot do, which others can. And everyone has a number of things that they cannot do. You may not be able to run 100 metres in the time that the person who will win gold at the next Olympics can. (You might respond that you have not done the training that the athlete who will win the 100 metres at the next Olympics has. But it is likely that, even if you did the appropriate training, you would still not be able to run that fast.) The difference between a 'limitation' and a 'disability' might be that a limitation is a lack of a non-essential skill, whereas a disability is the lack of a function that most people take for granted.

Of course, I would not wish to trivialise the matter by giving the impression that certain disabilities do not cause significantly more impairment than others, nor that such disabilities can always be 'overcome'. But we must all start from the principle that each person is an individual, with unique skills, talents and personality. No-one is defined by a disability. A person with an inability to walk is not a 'paraplegic', but a person who has a whole range of things for which they are valuable, but who cannot walk because of a syndrome that is conveniently summed up by the term 'paraplegia'. Similarly, people with diabetes should not be referred to as 'diabetics' or people with schizophrenia as 'schizophrenics'.

As we focus on putting people with disabilities back into the workplace, you should recall that there is now a whole raft of national and international laws demanding that people with disabilities do not suffer from discrimination at work. This does not mean that an employer has to employ someone who does not have the skills to do the job simply because he or she has a disability. What it means is that the employer should not refuse to employ, or continue to employ, someone who does have the skills to do the job, but who will have difficulty carrying out the tasks without certain reasonable modifications to the job and to the workplace.

The underlying rule for people thinking about the work of those with disabilities is that you should ask what skills are required to do the job and if the person has those skills. It may then be necessary to ask if any aspect of the disability interferes with the person's ability to do the task. It may be that the nature of the disability does not change, or that it changes as the medical condition (such as multiple sclerosis) progresses.

Having clarified that you have the proper skills and are able to do the job, despite your disability, you need to ask what obstacles need to be overcome by you and your employer to make it possible for you to work. There are two basic types of obstacles:

- physical
- social and interpersonal.

In many ways, the physical obstacles are more straightforward to overcome. Specialist technical advice is available and you should insist that it is accessed if you and your employer cannot find solutions. These can include adaptations to make the building more accessible to you (the entrance, moving around the premises and toilets) and to help you gain access to required work information (manuals, workplace instructions, electronic information). You should, of course, be able to evacuate the building in an emergency — so if you do not hear adequately, a fire alarm could be linked to a specially designated light that comes on in an emergency. Adaptation of the job will include both practical objects; the work station, tools, etc — and the job description, with work schedules that are appropriate for you and performance requirements that are attainable.

The social and interpersonal aspects start with you. If you show that you are confident in your abilities, and your confidence is well-placed, then others will share it. (Though this is also true of workers without disabilities.) You have to decide that you are content with how you are and that if anyone else does not like your disability, that is their problem. You do not have to apologise for their feelings and uncaring response.

There are, of course, a wide range of disabilities, and we can only touch on broad principles here. But the basic message is — even if you have a disability, whatever it is, it does not have to prevent you from doing the job that you want and for which you have the skills. Go for it.

Looking after relatives

As people in the West live longer, more and more of us are going to have elderly relatives. Although, nowadays, many people are highly active well into their seventies and eighties, not everyone is. It means that you may well end up feeling that you have to look after someone, such as a parent or perhaps an aunt or uncle. Or you may have a spouse or sibling who needs chronic care. It may be your spouse's parents — especially if you are the woman in the relationship — or a child who is chronically ill (though we will not consider looking after a sick child here).

But whether you plan it or whether you end up with it, you may find yourself to be a long-term carer for such a relative. You may read this before it happens, or you may be reading it because it has happened and you have only just noticed that you are not happy about it.

Before we consider the difficulties, let us recall one important point about caring: many people do it because they want to and, of this group, a large number find it very fulfilling and rewarding. It may be that they are valued by the person they are looking after (the words 'thank you', sincerely spoken, mean so much here), or it may be that the carer is able to value themselves in the role they have and thereby feel good about it. Whatever your reason for caring, as long as you do it in a caring way and do not end up abusing the person you are caring for, it is always a valuable, if demanding, task.

There are a number of issues in looking after someone long term, especially if they are sick and need a lot of attention. The first is that it will require a great deal of time. This may seem obvious, but when you are considering taking on such a commitment – and you may be one of the people who has the opportunity to decide in the cold light of day before taking it on – there is a tendency to shrug it off and convince yourself that you can add it to the end of a working day. Bear in mind that carers who try to look after an elderly relative while juggling a job and bringing up children have a greater risk of depression, chronic illness and reduced quality of life.

If you do find yourself caring for a relative long-term, make sure that you look after yourself. You may not get enough sleep; you may eat poorly; you may not do as much exercise; you may not go to bed when you are ill or to the doctor when you need to. And you may be tempted to ease the stress by smoking, using alcohol, or even other drugs.

Whatever the cause of your parent needing help, you must make sure that you have time to yourself, that you get breaks, and that you get what help is available. If you have a parent who is suffering from dementia, do not think that you cannot get any help from organisations such as the Alzheimer's Society and other voluntary bodies. Even if you are a consultant in old age psychiatry, you can still find such self-help groups useful. And make sure that you get every type of help to which you, or your parent, is entitled. As well as self-help groups, you may ensure that they get any benefit to which they are entitled. You may go with them to the GP to ensure the GP gets a good history; but remember your role as an educated lay person: the GP gives the medical advice, not you. Also, you may need to get legal advice about a power of attorney.

If it is a parent you are looking after, do not fall into the trap of thinking that you are now being the parent in the relationship. Even if you are having to do the most intimate tasks, such as changing incontinence pads, you are still the caring daughter, not the mother. You can consider yourself 'paying back' your mother or father for all the years of kindness they gave you. They helped you when you needed it (because you were a baby, infant and teenager) and now you are affectionately helping them.

But he or she is still your parent.

This is just as important if your parent is not demented, just frail. It may be that your parent is as frustrated by needing care as you are to provide it. And if your parent has been used to guiding you, it can be very distressing to them to find that you are now the one who controls what happens. It can, however, be helpful to you both to acknowledge this — your parent may be less distressed and you will not find that you are looking after someone who is permanently irritable.

If your parent is still in good shape, but needs a little support now and then, remember that you do not have to do everything. There is a tendency for a carer to feel this. But your parent may still have a number of good friends alive, who are not only able but happy to maintain contact. They may well enjoy spending time with your parent and vice versa — so don't feel guilty, when they come round, about having some time off.

The stresses on you will include the demands on your time, which will be many, and the relationship you have with that parent and other members of the family. If you have always had some difficulty in your relationship with your parent, you may feel some resentment for having to be the carer, especially if you have other siblings who do not seem to be doing as much for your parent. You need to stand back and decide what you feel you can do. You have as much — and as little — right as any of your other siblings not to care. Another sibling may live far away, but that does not mean that they do not have the same amount of responsibility for your parent as you do. They may have more difficulty fulfilling that responsibility, but you are entitled to ask that they work out a way of making an equal contribution, though it may be of another type; such as finding the money for two weeks respite care if you have been looking after your parent for the other fifty weeks of the year.

The important thing is that if you find yourself resenting caring for your parent, you should stand back and re-evaluate what you do have to do for your parent, and what you do not — and maybe jettison some of the latter.

If you are working, you will need periodically to review the situation and work out how much time you can allocate to each of the different responsibilities you have. You may decide that you wish to work part time, so that you have more time to do things for your parent. You may, conversely, decide to work full time and (money permitting) get someone else to look after your parent. Both courses of action are entirely acceptable — you just have to decide which.

Having decided how you want to order things in your life, discuss this with your manager at work. There are a number of ways that organisations such as the NHS can offer assistance to staff who have outside commitments; such as a reviewed working timetable and the option of having the occasional day off to deal with a crisis at home.

Despite the obvious demands, looking after an elderly relative can be very fulfilling, and you may find it easier to cope with the eventual loss of that parent to know that you gave them proper help in their hour of need.

Bereavement

The death of someone close to you may come as a sudden shock or it may have been long expected. Whichever way it happens, it is never pleasant. Clearly, if you have had some intimation that the person is soon to die, you will have had the opportunity to say goodbye. If not, there may be a lot unsaid.

If you are aware that the person is entering a terminal phase of an illness, you may experience a number of feelings that are similar to what is felt after death. You may feel irritable, upset and confused. You may want to spend more time with your relative and be less concerned with work and personal matters. It is important to be aware of this, especially at work, as your patients and colleagues may not be sympathetic to your moodiness if they do not know why.

Even if you were anticipating the death, you are likely to feel numbness on hearing the news that your loved one has finally died. You may not feel able to believe it — a mild form of denial. Although there is some doubt now that bereaved people go through five phases; denial, anger/distress, bargaining, depression/anxiety, acceptance, in a formal progression, you will at different times experience feelings from this list. You will have times where you feel miserable or angry for no reason, and then feel all right, only to return inexplicably to sadness. These changes may not have any formal triggers. You may also feel a yearning for the person, and you may think that you see them in all sorts of places, such as the street, only to find that it is someone else when you get closer. You may have sensations of the dead person's presence or even hear them say your name. None of this is pathological. The extent of how you experience the bereavement will be affected by the nature of your relationship with the person. If you were angry with the deceased, or ambivalent about them, it is harder to come to terms with the loss.

You will need to know the practical steps if you are left to sort things out. After the person has been discovered dead, you need to get a doctor (not yourself) to certify the death. If the deceased had not seen a doctor in the fourteen days prior to death, a postmortem is compulsory. When you finally have obtained the death certificate, you have to take it to the Registrar of Births, Marriages and Deaths. Only when the Registrar has issued his or her certificate can the funeral directors bury or cremate the person. Organising the funeral is complicated: you have to decide what you want at a time when you are feeling vulnerable. You are ripe for salesmanship. And costs are high — you can be talking in four figures. Have you got the money at a few minutes' notice? It may be that you will be waiting several days before you bury or cremate your relative, and you have more time to sort things out. You may also have to organise the social aspects of the funeral — inviting people, organising the reception (tea, wake, or whatever). At a time of feeling miserable, there is a lot to concentrate on.

One final difficulty at this time is that after death, all bank accounts of the deceased are automatically frozen. This includes joint accounts. The money cannot be accessed until probate has been obtained — you are advised to go to a solicitor for this. But it can take six weeks or more to get probate. If one of your parents dies, and the other survives, they may have to cope with several weeks without being able to pay a bill or buy food. No doubt a sympathetic bank manager will help, but at a commercial rate of interest.

If the relative you have lost is your first parent, then you may have to adapt to a role to the remaining parent that is significantly more supportive. If it is the second parent, although you will have been through this before, you will now have to face the fact that you are now the generation that is next in line. You have to cope with this while you are concentrating poorly and feeling vulnerable yourself.

In normal bereavement, the feelings ease over time. If you have loved the person, you will never stop missing them, but the pain diminishes, being briefly worsened on anniversaries and birthdays. As far as work goes, you are likely to have told your manager quite quickly, and few people object to colleagues being told. There may well be a policy for some compassionate leave, so that you can make the arrangements and attend the funeral. When you return to work, remember that you will still not be concentrating fully for a short period, and you should try to work at less than full capacity if that is realistically possible.

4

Management skills

You may have to stifle a yawn here: 'I came into medicine to treat patients. I'm not interested in all that management nonsense'. Well, you may not be interested in management, or organisational management, to distinguish it from clinical management, the bit you are interested in. But let me ask you a question: how do you treat a patient without a hospital building, a clinic, chairs and tables, examining couch, paper, case notes, prescription pad? Perhaps even a pen? How do the patients know where to come and at what time? And are you planning to see the patients for nothing or do you want to be paid?

Because if you are going to have a job in which you see patients, someone has got to do all of those tasks, and a whole lot more. And it is not one person, but a whole army of people. What they have to do may seem dull and routine, but if they don't do their tasks, you can't work as a hospital doctor. And there are certain tasks that you have to do as your contribution to the functioning of the hospital, beyond seeing patients and exercising your magic. This chapter considers some of the management skills that you will need.

There are two groups of skills that we will consider here. The first group consists of what might be called 'self-management'. In broad terms, if you are going to do a job, you have to have certain skills to make sure that you are fit to do it.

You are a resource. Cold though the phrase sounds, the reality is that if you are employed as a doctor for eight hours a day, then your employer has eight hours a day of medical time. If your employer employs two doctors, he or she has sixteen hours a day, and so on. Given the number of patients needing to be seen, and the time each patient requires, the hospital may need (say) eighteen hours of medical time a day in a specific department. You provide eight of those hours. There are a lot of demands on those hours and you need to make sure you use them as effectively as you can. There are certain techniques of time management, and we will look at them here.

If we look at the situation I just described, what do you think the employer, who needs eighteen hours of medical time, will do? He or she only has sixteen hours! The answer is obvious. Ask each doctor to work for nine hours rather than eight.

But there's a catch. The employer has a fixed budget. He cannot pay for the extra hour. Are you prepared to work nine hours and be paid for eight? If you are, will you work twelve hours and be paid for eight? Or eighteen hours? The hospital can employ you alone and the manager can use the money he would have used to pay the second doctor to have a lovely holiday!

The appropriate answer is that you should work, more or less, in accordance with your contract. Of course you will finish off a meeting with a patient, if that takes you five or ten minutes over your finish time. But you should not regularly work an extra hour a day.

How will you respond when the manager comes over to you with a sob story and tells you that he needs you to work nine hours for eight hours' pay? Of course, you could express your delight at being offered this fabulous opportunity to perform a wonderful public service. But if you do not feel such enthusiasm, how do you decline your manager's offer —especially if it is delivered in a bullying way? You could give him a punch on the nose, but that would mean that you would not work any hours as a doctor, as you would be promptly dismissed. So you need to be able to say 'no' firmly, but not aggressively; in doing so, you would be acting assertively.

But even if you can handle the people, the demands are still there. Whether you like it or not, there will almost always be more demands on you than you can possibly meet. You will feel under pressure. You need to know how to cope with stress. Stress is not a failing in inadequate people, but a normal response to excessive demand. **Some** stress, as they say, is good for you. But you can be sure that those who say that they thrive on stress are either not pulling their weight, or they are lying. There is a lot that you need to do to look after yourself. Applying self-management techniques can make a great difference to your quality of your life.

If you are working in a large organisation, such as the NHS, you will, whether you like it or not, have to work with other people. You will need a set of technical managerial skills (the second group I was referring to earlier). As well as your own ability to work with other people, you have to use the structures that help the organisation to get things done. These involve a series of groupings, mainly in the form of committees. Some groups are work related (ie. clinical); others involve the running of the organisation. You have to be able to take part in both types of group. You have to know how the groups (especially committees) work. You may even have to lead their meetings. You have to interact with other groups, and know how to negotiate with them. A typical example is a junior doctors' committee. You may find that the managers or senior doctors are pushing for the junior doctors to take on some additional task. How do the junior doctors respond to ensure that they are treated fairly?

You may be required to present all sorts of information; case conferences, journal clubs, research presentations, junior doctors' views to the trust management. You need to know how to present this information skillfully and effectively. And your use of a computer system to present it is only one of several IT skills that you will need in the course of your training.

Time management

Once you have signed your contract, you have agreed to provide yourself and your skills for a certain amount of time, usually eight hours a day, forty hours a week. As a doctor, you may also have agreed to provide an on-call service. That is — or should be — all the time you give to your work.

But somehow it never seems that there are enough hours in the day to do all that you are asked to do. How do you manage to fit it all in? The answer is that you manage your time. Nice-sounding phrase, but what does it mean? It means that you use the hours as effectively and efficiently as you can — and then go home. If there are things that haven't been done, that's just too bad.

As a doctor, you may well be shivering with fear at this stage. You know as well as I do that it feels almost impossible to meet such a counsel of perfection. With all the patients you are responsible for and the emergencies and millions of tasks that you have to do, you no doubt feel that there is no way that a busy doctor can leave on time. Well, let's deal with a few of these issues now.

First, being a doctor is no different from any other job when it comes to pressure. At the present time, many doctors do long hours, including on-call, but so do legal-aid lawyers, emergency gas fitters, single shopkeepers and workers in a whole host of other trades. There is nothing special about medicine, and it is well to accept this.

Second, we must be sure what we are saying when we trot out the extent of our workload. We all know that doctors have to see hundreds of patients daily — or do we? I once met a doctor who told me that he saw forty patients in the morning surgery, did twenty home visits, and then another forty in evening surgery. No doubt, if he'd continued, he would have told me that he then was on-call all night every other night and perhaps also had a job as a tooth fairy on the side.

But, assuming that he was not just boasting, what was he telling us when he said he saw so many patients? Yes, the number one hundred is large, but if we divide that into the number of hours in the day, we can easily see that he could, at most, have given each individual patient no more than one to two minutes. So we might wonder what he did for those patients in the thirty seconds between welcoming them in and ushering them out. In other words, we are asking what his job was and how much time each task really took.

Now, I am not saying that he was wrong in what he was doing. It just depends what he thought his job was and what needed to be done to fulfil it. Maybe one minute was enough to make the sort of interventions his patients needed; for example, many of the people who were consulting him may have been showing him a rash that was easily diagnosed and which did not require more than diagnosis and reassurance. Or, they might have been well-known patients requesting repeat prescriptions of inhalers for asthma? And it may be that that was all the patients wanted, so they went away satisfied. Or it may not have been the case, and some of his patients did not get proper diagnosis and/or treatment, and there was a large body of discontented patients whom he knew nothing about. It is impossible to know for certain.

However, when you are thinking about being under time-pressure, the previous case illustrates some of the principles you need to consider:

⌘ What is your job? Not just its title, but what are the tasks that your job comprises? Ideally, these should be written down in your job description. (Do you have one? If not, you should request one.)

⌘ What is not-your-job? What are the tasks that someone might ask you to do that you do not have responsibility for? These are the things that someone might approach you for, but to which you need to say 'no'. Sometimes, it is ambiguous or unclear — if you are an SHO and the specialist registrar on the team is on leave, which bits of his work should you do?

⌘ How long does each of the tasks take? And how much time does that require each day; for example, if you are doing an outpatient clinic from 2.00 pm to 5.00 pm, and each patient requires thirty minutes, you can only see six patients.

⌘ What gets in the way of you doing what you have to do?

⌘ If you do the sums, and there are more tasks to be done than time available (eg. there are eight patients to be seen at that clinic), how do you deal with this situation?

⌘ As it is likely that you will have to leave some tasks on each day, how do you manage the things you cannot do?

When you take a job, you should be told the purpose of the job. When anybody employs someone else (for anything), they usually want them to do something, often a defined task or set of tasks. So, you might employ somebody to wash your car. You would expect them only to wash one car

— yours — and not your neighbour's (your neighbour might employ the person separately, but that's a different matter). You would also not expect the person to clean your kitchen as well, if you did not include that in the job. You might ask them to clean your kitchen as well, but the person would be likely to ask you for some more money. But if you thought that you had asked the person to clean your car and your kitchen, but he or she thought you had only asked for the car to be cleaned, one of you would end up disappointed. It is important to clarify exactly what the job entails before starting.

Sadly, this is not always the case. In the development of medical services — both in the hospital and in the community — there has been a tendency to create a post and then clarify the tasks afterwards. So you will find yourself appointed as 'SHO in psychiatry' or 'SpR in psychiatry'. But what do these terms mean (apart from an indication of your grade and experience)? What are the duties of an SHO or SpR?

You may respond that it is clear — but it is not. You may think that you have been appointed as a ward doctor, but usually the SHO is the doctor for the day-to-day management of the patients of only one consultant. More recently, each consultant has patients on more than one ward, so the role of that SHO is not as a ward doctor, but as a team doctor. If you are the team doctor for the patients under Dr Smith's care and you happen to be on a ward where Dr Brown has patients as well, but Dr Brown's SHO is not around, do you cover for Dr Brown's SHO? What happens if one of Dr Brown's patients needs urgent attention and no-one else is available? If you do treat one of Dr Brown's patients, and get it spectacularly wrong (let's say that you were not aware that a particular patient of Dr Brown was allergic to penicillin, but Dr Brown's SHO did, and because you wanted to be nice and 'help the nurses out', you treated the patient for an infection with penicillin and the patient subsequently died), would you be happy to take the wrap? Or even go to prison? Not an absurd comment in this litigious age!

You must be clear which tasks are yours and which are not. However inconvenient others may find it, you must stick to them. This does not mean that you will not on rare occasions help out, but be clear about what you are doing and make sure that it does not have a negative impact on the care you are able to give the patients that you are responsible for.

At the start of your job you should ask your line manager — for a junior doctor, this will usually be your consultant — for a list of all the tasks for which you are responsible. If you are in a training position, you must ensure that your responsibilities with respect to obtaining your training are also clarified.

Often the use of seemingly simple devices, such as timetables and diaries, will indicate clearly how you are supposed to fit in all your responsibilities. If you find that, after sticking to your timetable, there are things left over that you cannot find time to do, you should go back to your consultant or manager and ask them to help you. A good manager will go over your timetable and, if there are more tasks than time, help you stop doing things that you don't need to do (such as sitting in a meeting at which you make no contribution); prioritise the tasks that you do need to do — and drop any that are left over.

Make sure you avoid two pitfalls in this process. First, ensure that you do not make unrealistically small assumptions about how much time you need for a task, and if your manager agrees with you that you will drop a task, do not take on the responsibility for finding someone who will perform that task (or carrying on beyond a very short time, say, one to two weeks). Do not accept abusive statements from bad consultants or managers, such as 'The previous SHO used to do it' or 'No-one has ever complained before'. Politely state that what the previous SHO did is not your concern and that the fact that no-one has complained before does not mean that you are not right to raise the matter.

Second, always try to use objective statements as the basis of your argument: 'I am only employed for eight hours a day and there seems to be ten hours of work here' is more effective than 'Of course the previous SHO didn't complain, but that's only because everyone is afraid of your temper.'

Part of the process may be a re-evaluation of the tasks. For an SHO or SpR, this may be an additional training exercise. You may take thirty minutes to see each patient in the outpatient department, but your manager, especially your clinical manager (ie. consultant) may be able to go through what you do and advise you about how you might do it a little more efficiently. It may, after the discussion, become clear that, if you change certain things you do and omit certain others, you can see each patient in fifteen minutes and still achieve the appropriate goal for that appointment. In this way, you may be able to do more than you originally thought.

When you go through the process, make sure that you include all time costs. It is very easy to say that you will attend the ward round in the hospital at 10.00 am and then start an outpatient clinic in the community mental health team building across town at 2.00 pm, but if the ward round lasts four hours, how do you travel to the clinic and arrive on time? ('You don't' is an insufficient answer.) Do not forget either that, as a human being, you also have to eat, drink and have moments of rest. They must be built in to your timetable (even if not all are formally stated).

Although it may not be possible to include this when working in junior positions, remember that the effect of the body clock is that people function more or less effectively at different times of the day. You are not a machine that will perform at the same level for eight hours continuously. You will feel sharper at certain times of day, vaguer at others, and simply fatigued at others. If you are able to design a timetable that takes some account of your own natural rhythms, so much the better. Although, when there are sessions fixed for the team (eg. a ward round that starts just after lunch when you are likely to be at your most lethargic), this may not always be possible.

And when you go through this process, make sure that you look at your emotions. Some people find it hard to say 'no' because they feel guilty. And the guilt may continue, even after they have said 'no'. If you have acted appropriately, use the rational part of your mind to counteract your emotions, say to yourself something like, 'I feel guilty, but I must remember that I did actually do the right thing.' After you have done this a few times, you will find yourself able to say 'no' without feeling guilty. Whatever you do, do not allow yourself to say, 'No, but I'll do it anyway.' You will continue to feel overloaded, you will do things — and resent it. It is the worst of all worlds.

As human beings, there are other factors that can interfere with our ability to accomplish the tasks that we set ourselves in the day. We are social animals, and we like to interact with other people. Chatting with other staff members is good for team-building, but if it is excessive, it prevents us getting things done. Account for such informal talk when you are devising your timetable. There may be unexpected interruptions, such as clinical emergencies, non-urgent telephone calls (eg. from GPs or patients' relatives), or visits (such as from patients' relatives or pharmaceutical company representatives). If you find yourself regarding these distractions as 'undesirable' or 'intrusive', you are allowing your emotions to get the better of you. Take the emotion away by stepping back and deciding for yourself what intrusions are appropriate for your job and which are not.

In the case of calls and visits, you can always ask someone (preferably your team's secretary) to take a message and then agree to phone back or meet by appointment. In the case of a clinical emergency, you will no doubt have to attend to it. It may well make you late for going home. It is reasonable to accept this with good grace on occasions. However, if you find that you are regularly having to stay late because of emergencies, you should raise this with your consultant or manager. There may be ways you can deal with the unexpected that are better than what you are currently doing (eg. recognising which ones are not real emergencies). If the nature of the patients that the team treats leads to frequent clinical emergencies, your manager may have to accept that you may have to drop a regular commitment to free up the necessary time.

To manage your time properly, be clear about your job; organise your day and your week; arrange things so that you can get straight on with your job (eg. if you feel you need a coffee before starting, come in fifteen minutes early to have it); avoid unnecessary or inappropriate distractions; and keep to time (one excellent manager I knew not only stood at the door in the morning to check that staff were turning up on time, but also went round at the end of the day kicking people out, ensuring that they left on time also).

There will be occasional days when there are more things that have to be done than is possible. On those days, if you review all the tasks that need doing, make the judgement that none can satisfactorily be postponed and realise that there is no-one else suitably qualified available to do some of them — other than you. Making a positive choice like this will help you feel better about what you are doing. With all these techniques, time should become much more manageable.

Assertiveness

One of the problems of working in an organisation is that, when things are not clear, disputes arise. If you disagree with someone else (whoever it is and whatever the issue), you have three basic options.

The first is that you fight. You can have a battle with each other in which the aim is for one to defeat the other, and thereby start to exert 'power' over the other. There are various ways of fighting – you can abuse each other; you can destroy each other's work (eg. shred the other's essays) or reputation (eg. by spreading gossip); or you can be violent (eg. bullying or hitting). In other words, you are aggressive.

The second option is that you concede immediately (to avoid any conflict at all). You are quiet, meek and do what you are told. You may not agree with what others are telling you, and your experience is that what they are saying will not work, but you are so concerned not to have a fight — which you expect to lose anyway — that you simply give up. In other words, you are submissive.

The problem with these first two options is that most areas of work involve co-operation between people. In the caring professions, co-operation is crucial. Behaving aggressively or submissively are both unhelpful in situations where co-operation is required. Those who behave aggressively will get their way on most occasions, but will miss the opportunity to avoid mistakes because they do not heed the warnings of others.

The third, alternative option is to behave in an assertive way. Assertiveness is neither aggression nor submission, but a recognition that both people in any interaction are of equal value. They may be in positions of different status, such as a consultant and an SHO, or a foreman and a worker on the shop floor, but as people they are both worthy of equal courtesy and respect. It does not mean that one should assume that the SHO has the same clinical experience and expertise as a consultant, but that the interaction should always be dignified. The consultant should not treat the SHO with contempt or as a minion ('Do what I tell you'), but the SHO should not expect the consultant to be available at a moment's notice.

People usually start to think about assertiveness when they are in positions of lower status, but assertiveness is a technique that is appropriate for everyone. From your own point of view, and looking to become assertive, what are the things that you would want to consider?

The first thing is to acknowledge that, as a person, you are as good as anyone else, but no better. As a doctor, you have some skills that someone else — say, a plumber — does not. But, conversely, the plumber has some skills that you do not. It does not make either of you a better person. But it is very easy not only to think that one is better than others, but also to gain the impression that one is a worse person than others. The medical profession has come in for a great deal of battering over the last decade. (Not that a whole host of other trades and professions have not — think of how people in the UK currently view estate agents and politicians). People consistently print stories in the media about how doctors are arrogant, do not listen, and then make mistakes. They also have printed stories that doctors are still one of the most trusted of all professionals.

So how should you view yourself? The answer is that you should make your own valuation of yourself, and not simply accept whatever any other person says about you. That is not to say that you should ignore their observations, but you should evaluate what they are saying and come to your own view about it.

As a result of this you, like everyone else, should be treated politely. If someone makes an offensive comment — whether about your sex, race, or some other personal matter — you have the right to point out to them that they have just said something offensive. You should express it courteously, saying something like, 'I'm sorry, but I do not think it is relevant or appropriate to make statements that I do not know about motor cars/football/gynaecology simply because I am a man/woman' or 'I don't like the way you have just said that SHO doctors nowadays are more stupid/less committed than in your day.' You should try not to let such statements pass, especially as not commenting on such statements implies that you are tacitly accepting what the other person is saying.

And if this happens more than once in a conversation, you may find that the other person criticises you by saying, 'Will you stop going on criticising me?' — to which you might wish to reply that you are not criticising, merely pointing out that you have found several comments offensive; you have made the other person aware; and that you hope that he or she will not make further such comments. You should also state that you are merely asking him or her to acknowledge that you have the right to be treated with courtesy, just as everyone else does, including your senior. Should this not be possible to resolve in the meeting, and should you be planning to continue working together, you may wish to gain the assistance of an external agent — a manager, another colleague, or a trade union such as a BMA industrial relations officer. (It is always better to get it sorted out locally and in as low key a way as possible.)

You must, of course, make sure that when you are making assertive comments and protecting yourself, you are not overtly offensive to the other person. You should also make reasonable objective statements in a non-aggressive manner. It is neither appropriate, nor effective, to reply to the consultant who says that SHOs are more stupid than in his or her day that this is because consultants are more arrogant than ever before. Use a statement, such as the one above, in which you ask the person to withdraw the statement that you found offensive, as this does not include an element of retaliation.

The issue is that you can express critical comments, as long as it is done in a constructive manner. As a rule of thumb, you may wish to fall back on the tried and tested 'criticize the behaviour, not the person'. Telling your consultant, your SHO, your ward nurse, the cleaner, or anyone else, that they are a bad doctor/nurse/cleaner is always destructive. Telling them that you thought that they did not write the correct dose of medication or that they did not dispense the medication at the time on the prescription or that you can still see some dirt on the floor is acceptable. If you add some comment like, 'Excuse me for bringing this to your attention, but...', you are not being submissive, but acknowledging that the other person has opinions (I think that the dose is correct, the floor is clean) and stresses (I've finished this floor now, so I can get on with the other 300 floors I am supposed to do before I can go home), before saying that one thing was not, in your opinion, satisfactorily done. And if you criticise behaviour, and use objective language, other people tend not to feel offended (though they may still indicate that you are adding to their stress by a growl).

Respect should be not only for feelings but also for needs and resources. You cannot do the job if you do not have the tools — whether access to MRI scanners or a psychologist in the team, or simply the time to do all that is required. It is not necessary for you to feel that you should 'cope', ie. do something without the resources. For example, if you are aware that a clinical technique is outside your expertise, then you should not attempt it. It is very tempting to 'have a go', heroically, especially if the patient may die if no-one does anything, but an inexpert intervention may sometimes be worse than no intervention at all. It is not 'coping' to have a go and fail. You should feel able to state that you would be willing to attempt the task (assuming it is within your role), but that you cannot do it without the appropriate resources.

When you stand up for yourself in this way, people may respond in a variety of ways. One particular response is to show distress. If you say 'no' to someone (politely), they may become angry or upset. But that is their problem. If they respond with words that explain their distress, such as, 'If you won't do it, who else am I going to get to do it?', it is for them to sort out, not you. Do not change your mind and agree to do it simply because you think that will be the way to turn off the waterworks.

Saying 'no' can be very difficult — one trainer reported giving those who attended her course the exercise of forming the mouth into the right shape and then saying the word 'no' as a means of starting to get people used to saying it. But you must be able to recognise when you are unable to do something — or take on a commitment and then tell people that you cannot do it.

Within hospitals (and other organisations), there are always hierarchical structures, and there are some people to whom it is particularly hard to say 'no'. Dr Raj Persaud offers ten tips on how you can say 'no' without appearing to do so (see *Table 4.1*). People work together better in an atmosphere of courtesy and respect. Assertiveness is not just about making your life easier, but also about maintaining your own and your unit's morale, and providing a better quality service.

Stress and coping

Were you one of those who were brought up to believe that if you tried hard enough, you could do anything? If you were, it's time to qualify your belief. All humans have their limitations. Yes, that's right. There's only so much you can do. It applies to everyone, so if you think that you might have your limitations, but your colleague — who appears so successful, capable, good-looking, etc — doesn't, think again, and be reassured.

We had an old family friend, a GP, a delightful man who used to say, 'I know I'm not perfect. I can't play the violin.' And if you think about it, you will be able to list a whole load of things that you cannot do. But I am not trying to make you feel that you are a failure because you can't do everything. Neither can I.

Table 4.1: Ten tips for saying 'no'

1   Never say 'no' to armed gunmen or NHS managers.

     a) Say, 'Yes, but...' and appear positive. In this situation, saying 'no' invites a retaliatory response.

2   Play for time.

     a) Say you will do it but take so long about it that nothing happens, (eg. delay answers, consult colleagues).

3   Put the ball back in their court.

     a) Have they checked with everyone else who needs to be consulted?

4   Bury it in a committee.

5   Ask for clarification.

6   Ask for something you need from them.

7   Say it's a great idea, but point out that it means that you won't be able to do last week's great idea.

8   Say you have to work in a team and have to check with others. Then the 'no' comes from the team, not from you.

9   Say that if you are to do it, you will do it well, requiring additional resources.

10   Ask, if it's such a good idea, why everyone isn't doing it?

Persaud, *Hospital Doctor*, 2002

But we do live in a generation in which expectations are so high as to be absurd. When we try to meet those expectations, we will necessarily fail. And we will suffer from stress, which is exactly what many people do. Given that stress is everyone's lot, let's deal with one thing straightaway. Stress indicates that you have more things to do than you can do, but it does not indicate that you are a failure as a person. Nor, conversely, is being stressed a badge of honour. What is important is that you learn to recognise your own feelings of being stressed and that you take appropriate action.

'What do I have to learn for?' you ask me. But look at the number of people, both doctors and those working in all other trades and professions, who tell you that they are not stressed and that they are coping just fine, when you can see that they are about to fall over. Yes, that old term (of abuse?) 'denial' comes back to haunt us. Many of us have been brought up to minimise the effects of stress. It doesn't matter how we feel, 'we'll cope anyway' — with the result that those of us in the medical profession all have known colleagues who have come to work when they have a temperature, are sniffling, and look like death warmed up, because they were so badly needed. Was it right that they should risk passing on respiratory infections to their patients? Have any died this way?

Let's think about stress, what it is, and how to deal with it effectively. Human beings have demands made on them all the time. Some are physiological (the need to breathe, eat, excrete, keep a proper body temperature, sleep, deal with acute threats from possible predators); some are psychological (the need to deal with negative emotions such as misery, anxiety, boredom; the need to maintain self-esteem; the need to care for others, etc); and some are social/economic (social interactions, including the production of goods and services; or getting breakfast ready; wiping your child's bottom; turning up at work on time; ensuring that great aunt Fanny has enough blankets now the weather has turned cold; paying the bills; producing a poster for an advertisement, etc).

We have to respond effectively to these demands. If we do not respond adequately to certain types of demand, we die — such as when we fail to get oxygen into our lungs. Other types of demand do not necessarily lead to death if there is no adequate response, but they have adverse or undesirable consequences. If you do not respond appropriately to the demand of the electricity company for payment of your bill, you will find that your supply is stopped. If you do not bother to change your baby's soiled nappy, the child may end up with a rash or even a full-blown infection around its bottom — apart from the disgust that others will have with your child.

When it comes to demands, there is no distinction between the demands of home and the demands of work. It is still a demand whether we will be paid for meeting the demand or not. So when you come to looking at the demands on you, you need to include everything – not just the work demands – when trying to understand where your own stressful feelings come from. To deal with a demand, you must have the resources. The main resources are health, time, social capital (i.e. other people) and money. You obviously need to breathe in enough air into your lungs for enough time to be able to extract the oxygen you need to perform all the physical functions of life. But I will leave the physiological examples at this point and focus on the psychosocial.

If you have enough resources to meet the demands on you, then you will manage your life in a non-stressful way. Humans are built to perform better when there is some level of demand, rather than when there is little or no demand on them. More simply, we perform better when we are stressed than when we have nothing to do (when we get the additional stress of becoming bored). The ideal is to have a moderate number of demands on you, and then a period of recuperating from the demands, each day. In a stable society, this often equates to working during the day and resting during the evening.

For many people, this is not the case. Jobs are often set up as though they are the only demand on the person. Sometimes, the job makes more demands on one individual than his or her capacity for the day. And then there are other demands arising out of home life.

A large number of people have more demands on them than they can meet in a given time-period. It is this situation that is referred to by the term 'stress', though we really ought to use some additional term to indicate that the person has a pathological level of stress. By failing to distinguish 'stress' — the term for (a set of) demands on a person — from 'stress' — a person's response to the excess of demands on them over their capacity to meet those demands — the impression is given that there is no problem. (Listen out to the chat shows where one person says that their life is being ruined by 'stress', and another then pompously chides them by saying that they thrive on 'stress'. The word is being used in different ways. This might seem petty until we note that managers often allow themselves to fall into the same trap.)

But how do you know that you are suffering from stress?

(From here on, I am going to use the term 'stress' to mean the human response to an excess of demands over capacity to meet them: in other words, having too much to do.) The answer is that your body tells you. If the stress is acute, such as when fifteen people are all clamouring for your attention at the same time, you may feel irritated, tetchy and resentful. You may find that you are giving snappy answers — trite and simple. They may not meet the needs of the person asking you, but they get them out of your sight. You may walk faster, speak faster and listen less. If you have enough self-awareness at a quieter moment, you will look back at yourself and realise that you were quite rude.

There are some people who will look at that description of the busy person and feel proud. 'Kicking ass' is one phrase that comes to mind. But be under no illusions: such behaviour is great for making your business fail. You are at high risk of taking decisions with insufficient information and, as a result, getting it wrong. In the case of medicine, you just might kill a patient. (Nowadays, society is less tolerant of arrogant errant doctors, and you may well have plenty of time to reflect in your prison cell.)

For those who have lived with stress for some time, they will complain of a number of things: constant headaches; migraines; stomach pains and bloating; constipation; back pains; a feeling of being tired all the time; feeling miserable; loss of energy; loss of interest; loss of enthusiasm in your work; loss of motivation; a tendency to get colds and difficulty shaking them off. Certain medical conditions can be precipitated or aggravated by stress — coronary heart disease, Type II diabetes mellitus, and peptic ulcer among them. And people will tell you that you have changed — you are not the lovely person you used to be.

So what can you do about it? The first thing is to recognise that you are suffering from stress. Of course, if there are one or more physical symptoms, you are right to ask your doctor to rule out obvious physical pathology. But once the basic tests have been done and your doctor is convinced that there is no physical disease to explain your symptoms, accept that you may have a psychological condition. You must also ensure that your doctor distinguishes your symptoms from depressive illness. Some of the psychological symptoms overlap, but in depressive illness, the cardinal feature is the predominant mood change that is out of proportion to external events. The distinction is important as treatment for depression is ineffective in the management of stress.

Try not to let yourself feel that the thought of having an emotional condition is so unacceptable that you embark on a fruitless quest for a non-existent pseudo-medical diagnosis, such as myalgic encephalomyelitis (ME, or chronic fatigue syndrome), irritable bowel syndrome, fibromyalgia and the like. That is not to say that these conditions do not exist — they are clinical descriptions — but that they have such a significant psychological component that you might as well accept that it is not a straightforward physical illness and the physicians are unlikely to be able to do much for you.

In light of the stigma that society puts on the various expressions of emotional distress, you should recall that the response of stress (in the sense of a response to excess demand) is a vital protective mechanism for humans — of whom you are one. Use it.

Having recognised that you are suffering from stress, what should you do next? Let's start with what you should **not** do. You should not try and medicate the situation by the use of alcohol, painkillers or proprietary cold remedies. By all means do so now and again to get moments of relief, but recognise that that is what you are doing. Do not try and get through a week at work, when you should really be at home in bed, by the use of cold remedies. If you are not fit for work, you should not go into work. No-one is indispensable, and your managers should ensure that your tasks are appropriately covered. For many people, this will be associated with a worry that there will be no job to come back to. But remember, it is more expensive to hire and train a new employee than to provide effective support to keep an existing employee. For junior doctors, you should not fear an adverse reference, as the consultant should understand your job sufficiently to know that the organisation is responsible for making it manageable.

Having recognised that your problem is stress, you need to review your home life and your work life. You need to list all the demands on you and the costs. Some of them will not be avoidable. If you have a baby, you simply cannot leave it with a soiled nappy indefinitely. You will be advised to look for other people who might take the task on instead of you, but your spouse or partner might be just as busy and stressed as you are. You should mark on your list of demands and responsibilities those which cannot be ignored, delayed or given to someone else.

Those tasks that you do not have time for, you may have to drop. You may have to change aspects of your lifestyle as a result. For example, you may find that you can no longer fit in as many snooker games in the pub of an evening, and that you have to give up your place in the pub darts team or the church choir. I am not telling you that you have to make these specific choices, as ultimately what you decide to drop is up to you. But if you have been a member of the pub darts team for the last fifteen years, it is a part of your life, and if you decide that you can no longer continue it, you will experience a feeling of loss.

For the tasks and responsibilities that you cannot drop, you may be able to modify things to make them less stressful. There are several types of causes of stress: insufficient resources; interruptions with your attempt to do your job; difficulties in your relationships and emotional response; and the changing nature of the work environment. *Table 4.2* gives some suggestions of how you may be able to modify stressors at work (though you should give equal consideration to the stressors at home).

The stress response is one that, physiologically, prepares the body for action. It follows that if you use up some of that mobilised energy, in the form of regular exercise, you will reduce your risk of suffering damage from stress. Sometimes it is possible to be efficient in stress management, for example, some working environments provide gyms on site, so that staff can exercise soon after work and at no extra cost to themselves.

You should frequently review stressful episodes and events. What happened and why did you feel stressed? How did you handle it? What can you learn from it?

As a footnote, remember that, just as you experience stress from all the demands on you, so do others. The mother in the post office queuing up for benefits with her three children (unruly or not); the nurse on the ward or in the community; the secretary who types for you (and 3000 other people) and the manager you go to for help with your problem at work — all are just as likely to be feeling the effects of stress as you are. Be considerate! Dumping on others because you feel stressed will not help anybody.

Table 4.2: Sources of stress and suggested solutions

Sources of stress	Suggested solutions
Insufficient resources	
Insufficient time	Time management
Insufficient money	Request additional funds
	See where other funds could be reasonably diverted
	Agree to do less
Insufficient number of colleagues	Request additional staff
	Agree to do less
Insufficient rest	Pencil rest times into your diary
Interruptions	
Interruptions – telephone	Get someone else to take the call
	Insist on phoning back
Interruptions – people	Politely refuse to be interrupted (unless clinical emergency)
Technology going wrong	Be aware that much of your work is dependent on technology and anticipate that there will be times when it fails
	Try to anticipate what technology might go wrong and make adjustments in your timetable to allow for it.
	Have systems in place to repair quickly
Speed of communication	Easy access (mobile phone, e-mail) increases demand. It does not all require immediate response
Negative emotions	
Negative interactions with others	Work colleagues are not friends. If someone irritates you, work at a practical level. Do not get personal. Do not harbour grudges
Expectations of others	Check that your requests are realistic
	Do not set someone else up to fail
Bullying	Assertive responses
Poor communication	Pay attention to:
	• ensuring you communicate clearly
	• clarifying others' communications to you
	Use all modes of communication
Organisational issues	
Low status/involvement in decision making	Very stressful. If you are of low status, you may have several peers. Talk to them and find joint solutions (may involve speaking to management as a group)
Organisational change	It is out of the individual's hands if a large organisation is undergoing a major change. The NHS has recently entered a period of constant change.
	Go with it, recognising that responsibility for outcomes during change does not ultimately rest with you

Interpersonal negotiation

If you have sufficient power, you can make people do exactly what you want. I am not going to go into the nature of power here, but if you do not have power over someone else, with whom you have to work either on a regular basis or for a specific project, and vice versa, then you have to have some mechanism for resolving disputes in a manner that is more or less acceptable to both of you.

We have discussed how you can assert yourself in situations of conflict. However, the process of reaching an agreement that both you and the other person can live with is that of negotiation. You may have to use negotiating skills for your own benefit, such as working out an on-call rota between you and colleagues, or on behalf of a group of people that you represent, such as a body of junior doctors, who might be in some sort of dispute with another group of people, such as the management or the consultants. In some situations, there may be formal dispute resolution procedures and policies locally, of which you should make yourself aware.

The first thing to bear in mind about a negotiation is that it is unwise to approach it as though it were a battle. It is not about winning or losing. If you (or the other party) approach it in such a way, the outcome is likely to be unacceptable to at least one party, and possibly both. And you will make it harder if you have to negotiate with the same people on a second occasion, as people who are smarting from a previous defeat may be less flexible the next time. You may have to negotiate in a formal situation, but you will also find yourself using techniques of negotiation in various other situations.

Negotiation — in the form of integrative bargaining (as opposed to distributive bargaining: see below) — is a process in which both sides try to understand what the other side needs and what the other side can concede in return. In an amicable negotiation, the aim is to find a situation where each side thinks that they have gained something — referred to as a 'win-win' situation.

The best background for a negotiation is where there is a good, long-standing, trusting relationship between the two parties. This is not always easy when you are in junior posts because, by definition, you will not have been in your post for a long time; and even if you stay in the same geographical neck of the woods on the rotation, you may not have more than a passing acquaintance with the managers, consultants and, sometimes, your peers. You should be careful not to confuse the popularity of a person with their trustworthiness. It is not uncommon to find that certain consultants or managers are popular or thought of as particularly nice (in preference to the others). You should try to find out the basis for their popularity. Does the local gossip network have reports of situations in which they behaved fairly ('She said that she would offer a teaching session at 8.00 am and she did') or where they behaved pleasantly but unreliably ('She gives great teaching sessions, but when she says come at 8.00 am, you can be sure that she won't turn up till until 8.40 am'). The latter person may be popular, saying the politically correct thing at meetings, making jokes that everyone laughs at, or just having 'charisma'; but if you hear stories that they are unreliable, you may anticipate that they may not support you when the chips are down. Of course, the gossip network may itself be unreliable, and you should be prepared to change your opinion in the light of your own experience, but you may use gossip as a guide.

So if you are asking for something (formally) from someone else, or the other is asking something from you, you should prepare yourself for the negotiation. Try and be clear what the issue is — sometimes the matter can appear quite vague. A start that the management wants to change the on-call rota is too vague. You need some idea of what is about to be proposed.

You will also want to know other relevant background facts. 'History' is often used against newer workers – 'We've always done it this way'. Is the claim true, or is it the statement of someone who has only worked there for a year, but it was changed two years ago? Custom and practice is important — it even has a legal connotation that we will not go into here — but you need to be willing to question whether the practice is established, and the basis for the practice. What was appropriate at one time may no longer be appropriate now that circumstances have changed.

You also need to be able to assert what your responsibilities are and what are the other sides. I once came across a situation where the study leave budget was, in numerical terms, significantly less than the contractual entitlement of the group of doctors in question. It is clearly the responsibility of the management to ensure that this budget is adequate. You will not be surprised to learn that statements were bandied about that 'The study leave budget needs to be cut' — why? What justification could there be for such a statement? — and that 'Study leave is optional' (which, in these particular circumstances, was not consistent with what was written in contracts). However, such statements can seem very convincing and you need to be able to examine what is being alleged to see if it holds water.

However, if the management were then to state that they could not meet the study leave budget, the doctors should not accept that they have a responsibility to make up for it. Some less scrupulous managers might try to encourage this. However, if an honest manager tells the doctors in good faith that he has a problem with the study leave budget — in that it cannot be increased at the present time to meet contractual requirements — it may be used as an appropriate bargaining tool: the junior doctors may agree to reduce their demand on the study leave budget in return for some other worthwhile concession.

(In writing this book, in the main, for doctors, I have given an example where management seems to be at fault. You should be aware that there are other situations where it is the doctors who are at fault. The point I am making is that it is not the case that one side is always wrong in different negotiations.)

In preparing for a negotiation, try to gain objective facts to support what you are going to assert, rather than opinion. The problem with a phrase like, 'The study leave budget needs to be cut' is that it is an opinion. It is by working out the figures that you can give substance to the opinion. (Who knows, in some other place, there may be a study leave budget that is greater than the contractual entitlement, in which case it would be reasonable for it to be seen as excessive.)

You should then get some idea of what you can and cannot do. Some people will refer to this as the 'resistance point'. In order to get the best deal possible, you do not tell your counterpart on the opposite side what this is, as you may be offered something that is better than you had hoped.

You also need to be clear what the relevant issues are to the negotiation you are going to have. For example, if there is a discussion about changing the medical on-call rota, then it is not relevant to talk about getting more nurses working in the day hospital or CMHT. Even if they are both important issues in their own right, do not bring in matters that are irrelevant. If you bring in discussion of two completely different matters, only do so if you intend to link them. Otherwise, it just blurs the picture.

Be clear exactly what you think is your best possible outcome and also the worst case scenario that you can live with. Also, be clear about what concessions you can make and what you cannot.

Try to establish what it is that the other side really wants (whatever it is that they *say* they do), and why they want it. If you have some idea of the pressure on them to gain what they are asking from you, then you are in a stronger position to ask for something that you want back.

In the negotiation itself, it is always better (if you can) to play fair. Do not be unnecessarily rude, and try not to get aggressive unless you have a good reason: you will have to work with this person you are negotiating with after you have reached a conclusion. People in more senior positions are better-placed to be rude and bullying. Try to distinguish the bullying of the negotiation from the bullying in general. In other words, some bullying, arguing and name-calling will only occur in the negotiation. You should remember to be assertive, not aggressive, keeping a low and gentle voice.

In the course of the negotiation, you should talk as though you are flexible and your mind is open to ideas, but do not automatically accept the ideas of your opponent; use the assertiveness techniques from the previous section. If you are abused, try to let it pass (unless racist or sexist, in which case gently disagree). Your self-esteem may be attacked, but you will help yourself by recognising the attack and handling it. Your opponent may describe you as 'intransigent', but you can say that you regret that he has interpreted your caution in this way and you hope that you and he can agree things more sympathetically so that you have a chance of getting a mutually acceptable agreement. Do not make concessions unless you feel you have got something back.

Assertiveness is also important, as you are more likely to conclude the negotiation successfully if you allow your counterpart to save face. If you embarrass your opponent, he will not be able to continue to work with you, and the negotiation will collapse.

By talking as though you are aware of your opponent's needs, you are able to ascertain more clearly what he actually needs, and you may be able to get to an agreement that meets the needs of both of you quicker.

Bear in mind that your counterpart and yourself may be speaking different languages. Your counterpart will have a set of goals that are determined by political need, whereas your goals will be driven by clinical need. The two do not match, but you will do well to see if these overlap. Once you have come to an agreement, try to get it down in writing. If your counterpart will not do that for you, then you may need to write your own letter recording what you thought was agreed.

The integrative form of bargaining that I have described here differs from distributive bargaining. In the latter, there is only so much of whatever you are discussing available. If you gain more, someone else must lose, and vice versa. This type of bargaining should be used with great care if you are going to work with the person again. Fortunately, this is rarely necessary in day-to-day NHS work.

Being on a committee

In all organisations, there are some decisions that can be taken by individuals, but there are others that affect so many people that they cannot necessarily be taken by one person alone. In a hospital, you may find committees to deal with:

⌘ The issues facing one particular group of staff (eg. the junior doctors' committee).

⌘ The development of policy for the whole unit (eg. a policy for dealing with visiting hours).

⌘ A committee to look at how a new service may be produced from existing resources (eg. a committee to work out how the unit may manage patients with two co-existing illnesses, such as learning disabilities and general psychiatry dual diagnosis).

⌘ The allocation of scarce resources (eg. a hospital medicines committee, to decide whether a given medication may be prescribed within the hospital, with special emphasis on new medications).

These examples are not exhaustive. Ideally, a committee should:

- be formed for a purpose
- carry out that task
- disband – unless it is a constant or monitoring committee.

A committee is not formed for people to meet each other (unless that is the specific task), to chat, or to escape other duties. The meetings of committees take up a large amount of staff time and should not be undertaken unless they are focused. Sadly, such a counsel of perfection is not always adhered to.

If you are asked to sit on a committee, you should begin by making sure what the committee is trying to achieve and what your role would be. Quite often, the person setting up the committee approaches people from a variety of disciplines (medical, nursing, paramedical, social work, etc) and sometimes people are taken onto committees because of their willingness to agree, rather than because they have a specific contribution to make.

If, for example, a committee is set up to provide an agreed protocol for managing acute behavioural emergencies in the A&E department, it is clear that, as junior psychiatrists are often involved in such incidents, the input of junior psychiatrists may be helpful. It may not be possible for all junior psychiatrists in the department to make themselves available for this task, so the selection of one individual — not necessarily the chair of the junior doctors' committee — to represent the views of the junior doctors is clearly helpful. However, if the committee is to decide on the nursing annual leave protocol, it may be hard to justify the presence of a junior doctor. These are clear examples to make the point, but other requests may require a little more consideration before agreement to participate is given.

If you are representing the junior doctors on a committee, you should recall that you are not just there in your own right. You may have your own observations to make, but you should also try to ensure that you obtain the views of all your junior doctor colleagues, as you will need to bring into the meetings views that you might not hold personally.

At each meeting, you should receive an agenda before the meeting and minutes (notes: a record of what was discussed) after the meeting. You should ensure that you have read the agenda and the minutes before each meeting. You should not be shy of making it clear in the meeting when the minutes do not meet your recall of what was actually said. For the agenda, you should ensure that the issues that are of concern to the people you are representing are raised.

As you are representing a role, rather than yourself, you should ensure either that you attend each meeting and that you are punctual, or that you have a replacement who has been properly briefed.

The work to be on a committee can therefore seem quite onerous. It means you have to review whether the effort you are putting in is worth it. If you (in your role) are able to gain something, then you should prioritise attendance, so that you can be on time. If you come to think that it makes no difference whether or not you are there on time, or what you say, you should ask yourself whether you should be there at all.

Chairing a meeting

If meetings are there to perform a purpose, as we mentioned earlier, someone has to make sure that the meeting functions effectively. This is the role of the chair of the meeting.

Being the chair is sometimes seen as a chore, and occasionally given to the person least able to refuse. But if the chair, and the meeting, are to be effective, they must:

- use the time available
- complete the agenda in time
- incorporate the views of all participants (if a person does not contribute, what are they doing there?)
- ensure there is an accurate record of the meeting (the minutes).

It is the responsibility of the chair to ensure that these tasks happen smoothly. It should be borne in mind that this can limit the ability of the chair to make his or her own contribution, and if there is one person whose contribution is particularly important, that person should not be the chair.

To ensure the time is used properly, the chair must attend promptly and must start the meeting on time. There is a tendency for meetings to start late when certain people are not present, but this is poor practice. Sometimes, it feels as though the contribution of one person is necessary before a decision can be taken. But the decision should be taken anyway, subject to modification in the light of that person's contribution. When the person in question arrives, their contribution should be brief. If that person tries to increase their contribution, he or she should be politely reminded that he or she was present when the time of the meeting was set and that he or she needs to make attendance on time a priority.

The chair should have a clear agenda, preferably printed, before the meeting. The time available should be divided by the number of items to calculate the time allowed for each item. (The only variation to this is when the committee has previously agreed that one item is of such importance that they wish to devote a disproportionate amount of time to it. The additional time should be specified and the time available for the other items reduced proportionately.) The chair should keep a close eye on the clock and be clear when it is time to move on to the next item. Objection may be made by some of the members, but the chair should politely but firmly remind the committee member that the whole agenda needs to be addressed.

There are a number of matters that can prevent the committee members keeping to time. Some people will speak at length. It is the chair's duty to interrupt and keep the person to time. The chair should note any deviations from the task at hand, such as a senior member who digresses into a reminiscence of how 'it wasn't like this in the old days, when old Fotheringay was here, then you knew what was what and...'. The chair should say how this may all be very interesting, but not strictly relevant, and ask the speaker either to make the point quickly or to stop talking immediately.

The chair should be watchful for repetition and verbosity. When a person is repeating a point, or if the point is being made using more words than is necessary, the chair should interrupt and try to summarise the point being made, with something like, 'We are running over time on this one, so am I right in thinking that the point you are making is...'. If the chair has paraphrased accurately, the speaker will be surprised that he is able to agree and will stop talking.

The chair must ensure that all the views that are necessary are incorporated. In most items, this will mean that all will need to make some statement. Again, the chair will have to divide the time available by the number of people who will speak and press each individual to keep to it. To achieve this, the chair will also have to deal with some of the matters going on under the surface. The participants in a meeting are usually of differing seniority, and some of the more junior members may be directly or indirectly intimidated by some of the more senior members. The junior member may be reluctant to talk, or reluctant to voice opinions contrary to that of the senior members. Despite the egos of the individuals, it is no benefit to stop dissenting views being aired, and the chair must work to make sure that everyone can say what they really think. The chair should not be intimidated, either, by the seniority of some of the other members of the committee in politely but firmly leading the meeting.

The chair should ensure that views are presented courteously and that overt conflict is not allowed to degenerate into overt verbal or (occasionally) physical violence. Statements aimed at individuals rather than at objective points must be headed off. The chair must step in when such conflict seems to be arising in the room and ask those involved in the row either to calm down or to leave the meeting. If the matters are particularly contentious, the chair can insist that all comments must be addressed to the chair.

The chair should discourage interruptions. Should someone indicate that they wish to make a comment, the chair should ask them to wait till he or she can find a suitable opening (usually, but not always, when the current speaker has finished). Indeed, throughout the meeting, only one person should be speaking at any one time. If others chat, while someone else is talking, the chair should ask them firmly to desist. The chair should be aware that private conversations in the course of someone talking is sometimes used deliberately as a destructive or discourteous technique. This prevents the meeting achieving its aims and the chair should be particularly robust in stopping such behaviour.

When each committee member has made his contribution, and the item is nearing completion, the chair should sum up and may at that time make a statement that may serve as the basis for the minute of that item. The advantage of doing it at this point is that committee members can be asked to agree to the minute at this stage.

It is useful for the chair to set the ground rules at the start, especially the fact that people will be stopped if they do not keep to time. After setting this rule, a verbose person who has exceeded his time can be told, when saying, 'but can I just say this', that his time is up and that he has missed the opportunity to make the point. Once this has happened once or twice, it will not happen again and the meeting will be the better for it.

There are a number of tasks that have to be accomplished outside the meeting. Someone has to be elected at the start of the meeting to take down the record of the meeting and to draw up a set of minutes of the meeting afterwards. Like the role of chair, this is not usually a popular one. The best option is to ask an experienced secretary to attend to take the minutes. The secretary is therefore assisted greatly by the chair's summary of the discussion and conclusion of each item. (The minutes should not be a verbatim record, but a summary of the main points.) If this is not possible, then one member of the committee should be selected. With the development of computers, it is now possible for the chair to record the minute as he or she summarises each item, though if this is slow, some committee members may not be tolerant of the delay.

It is sometimes entirely appropriate for committee members to communicate outside the meeting. There is a difference between a general meeting with many items and a discussion meeting. Some discussion outside the meeting can lead to the meeting only having to record the decision reached, rather than the discussion. A meeting in which a discussion is intended requires very few agenda items, so the matter for discussion can be properly aired and a consensus reached. Clearly, the discussion between members outside the meeting should not be subversive.

The chair should close the meeting on time (or earlier, if all items have been exhausted), indicating the date and time of the next meeting.

Although the reader might gain the impression that chairing a meeting is a tiresome task and that the role is rather petty, he or she will find that when meetings are well-chaired, the participants come out feeling that they have achieved something and that the meeting was not a waste of time.

Working with other disciplines

Another of those tiring-sounding, politically correct topics, I know — but this has more meaning than you might think. You are a doctor, and you know what your job involves, right?

Wrong. You know what you **think** you are supposed to do. But others may have a completely different view of what you are supposed to do. And they will tell you in no uncertain terms when you don't do it. Leaving you with two choices — an argument or a sulk.

The health service is full of a range of people with a variety of skills, approaches and contributions. There are other health and allied professionals: nurses, social workers, psychologists, physiotherapists, psychotherapists, occupational therapists, pharmacists, dieticians, porters, patient advocates, etc. And a wide range of administrative and supportive staff: organisational managers, secretaries, chaplains, estates staff, gardeners, painters, plumbers and electricians, payroll staff, patient volunteer services, etc. Invariably, at different times, you will come into contact with individuals working in most if not all these capacities. And you have to get on with them. The days when anyone can say, 'I'm the doctor — people have just got to do things the way I say' are well gone, if they ever existed at all.

From your point of view, what you do is important for patient care.

However, from the patient's point of view, what you do is only one of several important tasks.

You therefore need to know about your role and the role of other professionals. Having clarified in your own mind what your role is, you should tell the people you are working closely with. For people who change their job every six to nine months, as junior doctors do, this is a major task that needs to be done quickly at the start of each posting. You may not be sure at first what is expected of you, but the nurses will have an idea from your predecessors. You need help at your induction to understand what your task is — and what it is not. A quick way of telling people early in the job is by producing a timetable. You may have commitments that your predecessor did not, eg. you have a patient for psychotherapy and need to attend supervision on Wednesday afternoon. Your predecessor may not have had this commitment, and the nurses may have grown used to having the SHO available on Wednesday afternoon. They will be irritated if they find a resource they value removed without notice — so, by indicating when you will and will not be available, they can be advised of the need to adjust their expectations. Having published a timetable for your colleagues, tell them in team meetings what you will and will not be doing. You may need to negotiate some changes.

Similarly, you need to gain some understanding of the jobs of others and how they see their work. You may think that a nurse works under the direction of a doctor, but this is far from the case nowadays. Many nurses are highly experienced and work independently. Often they are community nurses or specialist nurses, and they may report back to a team, but not to a doctor. This does not mean that such nurses will not seek to discuss cases and obtain advice, but they will need guidance rather than instruction. You do not need to teach them the basics and you do not need to answer their queries: often with an experienced nurse, the role of the team supporter (especially a doctor) is to listen carefully to the nurse's account of the problem. The nurse will almost certainly have started talking about the solution by the time he or she gets to the end of telling you the problem, and your job there may be to ensure that the proposed solution does not have any obvious difficulty (most of the time it will not) and to support the nurse in the course of action they are already proposing.

You must also be aware that different disciplines will approach the same problem in different ways. The most obvious example is the difference between the doctor and the social worker, but there are differences between all groups. Often the differences are subtle, and you should be on the look out for situations where it appears that you and a colleague have the same viewpoint — but actually you do not, owing to small but crucial differences.

To use the example of the social worker, you may have a clear view on the management of a patient, such as a recommendation for compulsory admission. The social worker may feel that, although he or she understands your concern for the patient's immediate welfare, the situation does not warrant the loss of liberty that a compulsory admission involves. As a doctor, your interest in this situation is to gain control of the patient's symptoms — the correct approach for a doctor. The social worker may well come from a civil liberties perspective — an appropriate concern for a social worker. When you and the social worker are discussing the case, it is important that you are aware that you are coming from different perspectives and that your priorities are different. You should be careful not to personalise the matter, especially as you try to resolve the conflict in the situation I have described. Accepting that someone else has a different point of view does not, of course, mean that you have to agree with them. But when you disagree with a colleague's point of view, you should be careful not to use abusive or rude language.

Having a clear view of how other people view their jobs also helps you get an idea of what particular skills and competences they have — which you will then be able to access on behalf of your patients. You may believe that a particular patient would benefit from taking a depot neuroleptic and propose prescribing it. You may well find that one of the community psychiatric nurses has already got a relationship with that patient and can persuade him or her to accept the depot.

There are sometimes formal ways of finding out what your colleagues' jobs entail. You may be given a formal introduction to the unit, and (rarely) there may be a written description of each staff member and their roles in a pamphlet or brochure. But do not ignore the informal channels. When you find yourself sitting with a colleague, especially one whom you expect to have regular contact in the course of your job, ask him or her about his or her job. Even if you have previously met somebody working in a similar role, you should not make assumptions. For example, the ward manager on your present unit may see the role very differently from the ward manager on the unit you have just come from.

Talking to colleagues informally also presents you with the opportunity to develop positive and effective working relationships. Relationships at work can sometimes seem confusing, as you need to get on with people without overstepping certain marks. There will occasionally be someone you meet at work who becomes a close, long-standing friend, even a romantic partner. But for the majority of staff colleagues you encounter in your day-to-day work, this will not be the case.

Having recognised that, you must be clear about the nature of a working relationship: you must show enough warmth, goodwill and trustworthiness to enable your colleagues to feel that they can communicate with you, while keeping your personal life private (except for things that impinge on your working life, such as the birth of a child or a chronic disability). You do not have to invite people to your home; see them outside hours (eg. in the pub after work); or buy things for the workplace (eg. biscuits for the unit) unless, of course, you want to. But it does help if you know the names of the people you work with (including junior nurses and ward cleaners) and a little about them — if they are married, have children, what their hobbies are (if they are willing to disclose such information to you).

Generally, if you acknowledge colleagues with a smile or a greeting, you will find them more sympathetic to you. If you have a minute, talk to people rather than just ignore them. The subject matter can be superficial — in recent years, the topic of football is a very useful, non-contentious subject that crosses all sorts of social groups — but the aim is not the content of the talk, but the communication with another colleague. It may, however, be that your informal talk — in the kitchen making a coffee, in the staff canteen, in the corridor — is with a colleague with whom you work closely, and either or both of you may be grateful for the opportunity to discuss something important related to work (though ensure that you do not break patient confidentiality in such conversations) in a more informal way.

Having got to know individuals, you will also need to know the teams that you work in, and how they work. Most probably, you will be involved in a ward team and a community team, under the guidance of a single consultant, though you may find that you have a number of other teams that you join. Each team will have an ethos and a set of principles. They will not be written down, and you need to learn them quickly from current members. For example, the team may meet for a ward round every Tuesday. In some teams, all patients are discussed; in others, only those causing concern to the team member present are discussed. There is no right or wrong about it — you have to learn the ways of each team you meet. And your way may not be their way.

It is also worth bearing in mind that teams change as personnel change — and, for a variety of reasons, this is now common in the NHS. What was a standard way of working two years ago may have been entirely discarded as different team members change. A definition of a team is:

> *... a group of individuals who work together to produce products or deliver services for which they are mutually accountable. Team members share goals and are mutually held accountable for meeting them, they are interdependent in their accomplishment, and they affect the results through their interaction with one*

another. Because the team is held collectively accountable, the work of integrating with one another is included among the responsibilities of each member.

(Health Care Team Effectiveness Project, 2002)

Bear in mind that if you work in more than one team, the coherence of the teams may not be so easily achieved. However, there are some issues that occur in a well-functioning team:

- the goals and/or objectives are clearly stated
- the members show high levels of participation
- new ideas are encouraged
- There is good communication, with regular meetings, in which information can be shared, alternate viewpoints aired and resolved, and collective decisions made
- There is good leadership, in which the focus is maintained on the team's objectives, internal disputes are addressed, and the team is supported against external pressures.

One particularly useful tool in optimising team functioning is the use of an away-day. This is where the team withdraws service for a day and meets, preferably at a location off-site, to discuss issues of current concern. All team members should go, including those whose membership is time-limited. It is not a 'jolly', but an opportunity to address serious concerns. The use of a facilitator — an experienced person who will run the day — is strongly advised.

Presentation skills

Throughout your medical career, you will constantly be asked to talk to a wide range of people. On occasion, you may be asked to talk to a formal gathering; at others, you may be asked to talk to a group of people informally at a moment's notice.

You may be asked to talk to a group of your peers, perhaps at a case presentation (more senior doctors may be present); you may be asked to give a lecture to a group of medical students; you may be asked to present at an international research conference; you may be asked to explain to some managers why you and your colleagues cannot change the on-call rota as they were hoping you might; you might be asked to talk to a group of patients about the illnesses they are suffering from. Whoever you are talking to and whatever the settings, you need to know how to present yourself and your information.

In this section, we will think about preparation for a major talk, but you should bear in mind that you are on show every time you address any group of people. If, for example, you are suddenly asked to talk to a group of four visiting student nurses about the work of your unit, you still need to use the principles we will discuss below — though modified to meet the circumstances (lack of preparation time, lack of clear brief, etc).

When someone contacts you to speak, you must find out at that stage what it is that the person asking you wants. What is the meeting at which you will speak and why have they selected you? The answer to the latter question may be obvious — if the specialist registrar in Dr Blogg's firm gives the regular talk to the medical students on schizophrenia, and you are currently holding that position, it may be a part of your current post (in which case, you should ask if there is a regular content to the talk). However, on occasion, the reason it is you who is being asked may not be clear. Do check that the organiser who is asking you has got the right person. You do not want to find out on the day that the audience is expecting someone quite different — and the organiser simply confused your names.

If you are clear why the organiser has selected you in particular, you may get a clearer understanding of what you are being asked to talk about. It may be that someone heard you speak previously and recommended you. If so, the present organiser may be expecting the same type of talk. For example, if you gave a talk on living with schizophrenia to a group of patients, and then were contacted by someone from a self-help group, you could expect that you might deliver the same talk as last time. But if you find out that, after talking to a group of patients about living with schizophrenia, your next call comes from the secretary of the department of pharmacology, the chances are that you will be asked to talk about some more biological aspect, such as the pharmacokinetics of neuroleptics.

Having confirmed what you are being asked to talk about, you need to be sure in your own mind whether you are capable of giving an appropriate talk or not. If you are, you must clarify, at the first opportunity, the following matters with the person asking you to talk:

* What is the date and time of the proposed talk?
* Where is it to take place?
* Is it a single talk, or is it part of a conference programme? If it is the latter, who else has confirmed that they will speak? (It is not sufficient to know who the organiser 'hopes might be persuaded'.)
* What are the other talks on the programme?

⌘ How long do you have available to talk?

⌘ How many people will be in the audience?

⌘ What are their backgrounds?

⌘ What facilities will be available for your presentation (flip chart, overhead projector, computer projector, video, etc).

⌘ What are the financial arrangements? Will you be paid for the talk? Will you be paid expenses? Will the organiser make the arrangements for you?

You must ensure that you have enough time — from the call requesting your attendance to the date of the presentation — to prepare adequately. You should start preparing early, especially if you have to collect new data or illustrations.

You must design the talk in accordance with the needs of the meeting. If you have been given a forty-five-minute slot, you must not put so much information into a talk that you have no chance of finishing on time.

Start arranging your presentation by writing it in the form of a summary. What are the main points that you want to get across? You should list them and be able to say them in less than a minute. This can then form the spine of your talk, around which the rest is explanation and additional information. The amount of additional information can be tailored to the time available. The nature of the extra information will vary as the audience varies.

As a rule of thumb, it is suggested that the limited attention and memory span of all audiences is such that you should include no more than five to seven points or headings in a forty-five-minute talk. If you were asked to talk on, 'Drug treatment of depressive illness', you might have an outline as follows:

1) Introduction
   a) Depressive illness is common
   b) The diagnostic features are the following symptoms and signs
   c) There are a range of treatments: pharmacological, physical (ECT), psychological and social
   d) We are only talking of the pharmacological treatments today
2) Scientific basis for the use of antidepressant medication and evidence of its efficacy
3) Overview of pharmacological treatments
   a) Tricyclic antidepressants, selective serotonin reuptake inhibitors (SSRIs), MAOIs and RIMAs, lithium, others
4) Practical prescribing of antidepressant medication
   a) Selection of medication

b) Dosage
c) Managing the period for response
d) Side-effects and their management
e) Cessation of use

5) Summary

This outline could meet the requirements of a number of audiences. For a group of non-specialist doctors, you might spend a little more time on the section on the scientific basis for the use of antidepressant medication and you might want to include, for example, diagrams of the chemical structures of some of the compounds on your slides. Conversely, to a group of patients, you might pass quite quickly over the section on the scientific basis of antidepressant medication — though without missing it out — whereby you indicate that doctors prescribe such medication because of a scientific basis, not out of bigotry. In the patients' group, you might want to spend more time on the effects and side-effects of the various medications, and how to minimise them.

Having got the content of your talk clear in your mind, you should prepare some recall device for yourself and some presentational slides. Many people advise against the practice of reading from a prepared script. If you can manage to recall all you wish to say from notes, your slides or your cue cards, then that is desirable. However, if you do feel that you will only be satisfactorily prepared if you have every word available, then you should practice reading it in a way that does not sound stilted.

Audiences nowadays expect visual support for a talk. If you are involving the audience in a discussion, you may use a flipchart. Thus your presentation slides grow during the course of your talk. Otherwise, you should prepare slides, either on acetate for use with an overhead projector, or on a computer for use with a programme such as PowerPoint. You must check with the organiser that the appropriate facilities will be available. A good organiser will ask you what you want, but not everyone organises things perfectly. In the end, this is an example where, if you rely on someone who lets you down, you are the one left holding the can — it will be you standing in front of the audience, unable to proceed.

Slides should contain only brief pieces of information, to support your talk. They should not be the text of the talk. They should contain no more than three points and one image (graph, picture, etc). You can type directly onto a computer if you are using this method, and you can download pictures and graphics from the internet. You should bear in mind that such images will be subject to copyright. If you are presenting in a non-commercial environment, especially if it is an educational talk, you are unlikely to have to pay a copyright fee. However, if you are in a commercial environment, you should try to comply with the copyright rules. You should try and ensure that you can vary the appearance of the slides — even a PowerPoint presentation starts to get very repetitive and dull if all the slides have exactly the same appearance. You may wish to change the colour of the background slide or change the colour of the text. This can be put to advantage if you are dealing with different points or topics, as a change of colour can indicate to the audience that you have moved on into a different area. Make sure that your slides are legible. Not only should you limit the number of words per slide, but you should also use a font size no smaller than 18 and preferably significantly bigger.

There are various formats that people use for the structure of a talk:

⌘ Sequential – in which you go through a series of connected points to reach a conclusion.

⌘ Pyramid – in which the main ideas are presented at the start and repeated in greater detail through the talk. (This is useful if you do not know how long you will have to speak.)

⌘ Beginning-middle-end – in which there is an introduction, a main body of the talk, and a summary of what was said.

When you have completed the preparation of your presentation, you may wish to prepare a handout. If you are giving a talk in which you are trying to persuade others of your point of view, there may be little value in this. However, if you are giving a lecture where the audience will wish to review information you have given them, then you may wish to assist by providing a handout. This allows the audience to concentrate on understanding what you say, secure in the knowledge that the details — such as the spelling of new concepts and references — are available for them afterwards. A print-out of your slides (six slides per page) is often the most helpful way of doing this.

Despite your preferred presentation, you should also ensure that you have a back-up plan in case the projector you were promised does not materialise or the computer fails to recognise your disc. If possible, have two modalities of presentation available (eg. computer slides and acetates). And be sure of what you might do if the only option available to you is to talk to the audience unaided.

On the day of your talk, make sure that you continue to prepare carefully. You need to ensure that you will arrive in time, so be certain of the route and the address. Have with you the telephone number of someone on site, so that if there is some unavoidable delay (eg. your train breaks down), you can ring to say that you are going to be late. Make sure that you have chosen your clothes and that they are ready and clean. In choosing what to wear, remember that the audience will interpret your clothing accordingly. If you are trying to present yourself as a professional, there is no point turning up scruffily dressed. However good the content of your talk, the audience will draw the conclusion that you are not serious about your subject. Before you leave your home or office to go to the talk venue, make sure that you have with you all that you need (correct computer files, correct discs, correct acetates, etc) in the right order.

Aim to arrive with plenty of time. You will need to find the exact venue (lecture theatre, teaching room, etc) and to ensure that the computer/overhead projector/video is working properly. You should locate the organiser and the person who can assist if something goes wrong during the course of the lecture (eg. the overhead projector bulb goes). You should see that the equipment is working properly and that you have a proper screen to project onto. Check the lighting — can the room be properly blacked out and is the screen white and clear? Stand at the back of the room to see what your presentation looks like. If you are presenting at a conference, you should also try to locate the person who will be chairing your session and introduce yourself (if you do not already know them). You may wish to give them a brief resumé about yourself, which they can use to introduce you. Do not assume that a chair whom you have never met has any idea who you are.

Having done all this, you should see to your comfort. Go to the toilet and make sure that you have eaten. It is easy to ignore these in the excitement of waiting to present, only to find out that you are bursting or starving just as you are about to talk.

When it is your time to talk, approach the lectern confidently. You have done your preparation, and you know what you are going to say. This is a time for you to give a performance, not think off the top of your head. You may feel some anxiety, but you should channel that into a modest, but confident presentation. You should speak confidently, slowly and clearly, directly to the audience. Do not face back towards the screen. If you are using an overhead projector, you should face the audience and look at the projector. This can be a little uncomfortable, because you will see the light, but it can be managed with practice. You can also point directly onto the acetate. You should only glance quickly and occasionally at the screen, to ensure that the acetate is the right way round and properly placed on the screen – but then turn promptly back to the audience. If you are using a computer, it is possible to arrange it so that the slide appears both on the computer screen and on the projector — enabling you to look at the computer screen and over it at the audience at the same time.

If you have prepared accurately, you will finish your talk a few minutes early to allow time for questions. Do not allow yourself to run over, as the audience will lose concentration on what you are saying and start wondering how well the chair will restrain you. The audience will also think badly of you for not being able to plan properly and, however good the talk might have been, the audience will be left with a bad impression.

When you are asked questions, you should, on the whole, not get anything that cannot be handled. If you are asked a question, you either know the answer or you do not. If you do not — say so, and move on to the next question. Do not answer incorrectly or way beyond your knowledge or expertise, as you will look foolish. Sometimes a member of the audience asks a question that is really no more than a statement of their views. You do not have to reply if there is nothing to say. Simply acknowledge the statement and move on. If you get someone indicating strongly that they disagree with you, do not be upset. Remember that you are entitled to your view and the other person to theirs. You might deal with it by saying that you accept that they hold this view, but you do not agree with them. Do not try and argue the point in public (unless it is a simple factual matter) – it is better to offer to discuss it in detail in private after the session.

After you have come down from the lectern, making sure that you take all your presentation materials with you (you may want them for another time), allow yourself some time to regain your equilibrium and then spend a little time reviewing how the presentation went — what went well and what went not so well — so you can learn for next time.

Information technology (IT)

IT is changing the way people work. As a result of word-processing packages (eg. Microsoft Word), especially when combined with voice-recognition software, personal diary (eg. Microsoft Outlook) and e-mail, many of the functions of secretaries can now be handled by individuals. The NHS has been cutting back on its administrative support for years, so the change has already been factored in. But the point is that all workers in organisations such as the NHS are going to have to be able to use these IT packages. We will discuss what IT skills you must have, and how you might obtain them.

The essential personal skills that you need for work include those packages in Microsoft Office — Word, Excel (a spreadsheet), PowerPoint, Access and Outlook. You will also need to be able to use the internet. In addition to these basic packages, you will need to be able to operate locally used programmes, such as statistical packages for research, or clinical programmes, such as computerised prescription generation.

Increasingly, workers in the NHS have either individual or shared access to computers containing the essential packages. It has become a new function of library services to provide local courses on their use, and you can contact your librarian for details. Alternatively, you can seek help from various adult-education sources, though this may be outside office hours.

IT literacy is a skill that the NHS needs you to acquire, so you should discuss the major gaps in your knowledge with your supervisor and trainer. It is entirely reasonable to include attendance on such courses as part of your general training (it should be addressed with your course trainer as well as your consultant trainer for the present job) or personal development plan when you are in a permanent position (as a consultant or staff grade/associate specialist doctor).

It is worth bearing in mind that the best way to learn computer skills is to use the computer, and you should do what you need to on the computer as much as possible. If you write a lot of letters on the computer, you will learn how to produce higher-quality letters — with better presentation; the use of highlighting techniques (italics, bold, bullet points, etc); and headers and footers that allow your documents to be more safely recorded. For example, if you use a footer to put details about the letter — the patient and recipient, plus the date and page number — on every page, you can ensure that if your letter is mislaid or split up by the recipient, then it can be put back together at a later date.

Also, you can learn how to use the computer as a filing system. For example, if you save a file in the form 'Joe Bloggs', it will appear after 'Fred Smith'. If you want these patients in alphabetical order, then you need to name the files 'Bloggs, Joe' and 'Smith, Fred'. If you want to know which of several letters this is, then you could also add the date. Again, the computer will go in order of the numbers presented, so you should date a file 040622 (22 June, 2004) rather than 220604, as the latter will appear after 130904, not before. There are a whole number of other techniques that you will only discover as you use the packages. One additional point: you should consider learning how to type. There are a number of teaching programmes that teach typing.

You should also experiment with PowerPoint. When you start, there are 'wizards' — programmes that guide you almost automatically into producing a basic quality presentation. Wizards will give you an idea of some of the things you can do to make your slides look different from each other. Don't be afraid to experiment.

If you are not sure of your use of computers, remember to save anything that you do frequently. If you are writing a Word document, it is a good idea to save your document every paragraph. If something goes wrong (eg. the computer crashes), you have not lost your whole morning's work.

Also, try to make sure that you regularly save to more than one place. As well as to the computer's hard drive, you should always make sure that you have a backup copy on a floppy disc or a recordable/rewritable CD. Otherwise, you may do a major piece of work (such as a proposal or a thesis) and lose it when your only copy disappears. Saving frequently and to more than one place is a chore — but if you develop it as a good habit, there may come a time when you are glad that you did.

Frequently, you will find yourself working on IT equipment provided by your workplace. There are usually policies for IT use, and you should make sure that you understand what is permitted and what is not. Small periods of personal use of the internet are often permitted by employers, but not when this takes up a significant portion of the working day (though there will be employers who do not permit such use at all — you need to check your employer's policy). Accessing racist or pornographic sites is likely to be strictly prohibited. You should bear in mind that, if the trust has a policy, and you break one of the rules, you are committing an offence that can lead to disciplinary action, even dismissal.

Another issue for the employer is the requirement to meet the obligations of the Data Protection Act (1998). One aspect is that sensitive personal data required for use in (for example) medical contexts must be held securely – ie. with a password. If you are provided with a 'user name' and you have a password, you must not give this password to anybody else, not even a secretary, however much you trust them.

You should also be mindful that, although working at a computer feels like a private activity, everything that you do on it is recorded. In particular, you should know that files can often be retrieved after (you think) they have been deleted, and that e-mails – whilst a very convenient form of communication – will still be visible to others after you have left. Never write anything personal or offensive in an e-mail. If you bully another member of staff by e-mail, using racist, sexist, homophobic or other offensive language, these e-mails can be retrieved and used against you. Similarly, sending pornographic, racist or otherwise offensive jokes may seem a funny idea at the time, but can land you in the same difficulties. Even if you are writing mildly flirtatious e-mails that are acceptable to the recipient, you should recall that you are effectively flirting in public.

This is not to say that you cannot use e-mail to send warm greetings in the form of gentle wisecracks to sympathetic colleagues, or that you should refrain from saying, in an appropriate manner, things that need to be said. Just do not assume that what you say is forgotten once the 'send' panel has been clicked.

IT packages can be extremely useful. It is not possible to list all their uses, and no doubt many others will emerge over the next few years, but here are some of the programmes in Microsoft Office, and what you can do with them:

⌘ Word – a word-processing programme in which you can write letters, teaching material, ward protocols (especially various drafts, so that people involved can agree the protocol).

⌘ Excel – a spreadsheet programme in which you can insert and manipulate data; particularly useful for small audits, though you need to give some thought as to how the data you intend to review will be collected and inserted.

⌘ Access – a database programme in which you can prepare, for example, a list of people who might be on a mailing list for an academic programme, or keep a central list of local and national resources (eg. hostels, day facilities, sheltered work programmes, etc).

⌘ PowerPoint – a presentation programme in which you can make professional-looking slides at short notice for a presentation. Unlike acetates, the PowerPoint presentation can be altered on the day, if required.

⌘ Outlook – an e-mail and calendar programme in which you can send and receive e-mails, and store regular commitments and individual appointments. It is hoped that all NHS workers will eventually have their own NHS e-mail address that does not change, wherever they work.

You may also have access to the internet. There is a great deal of very useful material available. Working in health care, you should be particularly aware of the governmental and statutory documents that are available, such as the Department of Health's website (www.doh.gov.uk) and the legislation available on the Home Office website (www.homeoffice.gov.uk).

There may be a number of websites that are of particular relevance to you. For example, the website of the Royal College of Psychiatrists has a whole range of information about the college and examinations, plus access to the full text of its three journals (*British Journal of Psychiatry*, *Psychiatric Bulletin* and *Advances in Psychiatric Treatment*). One particularly admirable development is the Health Information for London website (www.hilo.nhs.uk), which permits NHS workers access to a wide variety of information, including abstracts or full texts of a great range of academic journals, allowing for the real possibility of people practising evidence-based medicine.

As well as general computer software, you may encounter local software. An example would be a computer programme that permits the generation and printing of prescriptions. You should get a proper introduction to the use of such programmes from your colleagues as you are inducted.

This section has been intended as a general introduction for those whose experience of IT is limited at present. We have not, for example, touched on still or digital photography and its implications for teaching, nor a whole range of other possibilities that IT brings.

5

Psychiatry in its social context

When you started at medical school, all you wanted to do was get on and treat patients (at least, that's all I wanted to do.) And when you qualify, you see your future in healing the sick, a respected pillar of the community, just like on those TV dramas.

As you get more experienced, you realise that it is not like that. Not that the medicine is not fascinating — it is, and the pleasure you get from seeing an ill patient, whom you have treated correctly, get better is immeasurable. But as you get more experienced in your chosen branch of the profession, you realise how much more you could do. And you start to experience the obstacles that stop you. Some of these obstacles are personal (you only have twenty-four hours in a day, and the demands of your family might be high, for example). But some are not; they are inherent in the system: the shortage of beds, the hostility (and sometimes benevolence) directed towards the medical profession by the media and, from time to time, the public. In short, you start to realise that you are not treating patients in an ideal world, with all that you need at your disposal — in fact, quite the opposite.

And you realise that these obstacles include the very things that you always said were not important to you; politics, money, prejudice of the public, fame. Whether you like it or not, medicine is part of society and you are affected by society's views. Although we would rather get on with the job of treating patients, we have to think a little bit about the context in which psychiatry is practiced.

We must think in simple terms (I am not qualified to think in deeper terms) about economics and politics, and how they show themselves in the medical sphere. In particular, you will notice that psychiatric patients suffer a great deal of stigma and, sometimes, so do their doctors, nurses, social workers and others who try to help this underprivileged group. We must also think about how services are structured, as this affects service delivery. Hospitals do not spring up overnight, and the community facilities vary in location and type.

Both politics and geography conspire to shape the services that can be provided. Much has been made of regional variation in healthcare delivery. Some of it cannot be avoided, given the widely differing structures. But the Government has tried to ensure that the NHS, at least, has a chance to work towards comparable standards across different regions by insisting that service providers look to provide the best service they can — by rooting out unnecessary, bad or sloppy practice, by the process of 'clinical governance'.

The aim of this chapter is not to persuade you to become a medical politician, a media campaigner against psychiatric stigma, or your trust's clinical governance champion. Rather, it is that you should gain an insight into the system you are working in, so that you do not spend all your time railing against the injustices of the system that cannot be changed — and that you have a chance to influence things, even in a minor way, when and where you can.

Introduction to economics and politics

Imagine that you are the junior doctor in charge of the psychiatric SHO on-call rota for your hospital. There are five SHOs, one of whom works part-time. How do you construct the rota?

Simple, you reply. Put each doctor on-call every fifth night. But did you mean that? How often should the part-time doctor be on-call? The same as the rest, or proportionately less?

And what about the weekends? Do you put people on-call every fifth night, or do you limit that to every fifth night during the week and every fifth weekend?

And is a weekend 9.00 am Saturday to 9.00 am Monday, or is it Friday to Monday? Or do you have one person do the Saturday twenty-four hours and another do the Sunday twenty-four hours?

And we have not even considered the European Working Time Directive. How do you ensure that everyone has the proper amount of rest?

And what do you do when one person says that they must have a particular weekend off (say, to go to their sister's wedding), but no-one else is available to swap?

The problem that we have described is a political one, based on the economics. You, as the organiser, have a limited set of resources — five doctors. You have to deploy them, within a set of external constraints, to cover a certain task: you have to make a decision about how they will be deployed. Let us suggest the following descriptive terms:

- economics quantifies the resources (goods and services) in a society
- politics is the means by which the society chooses to spend/allocate those resources.

The resources available to you for the rota are four-and-a-half doctors (assuming that the part-time worker is working half-time). In financial terms, this represents a budget of four-and-a-half doctors' salaries. If you are the manager, you might have a little more money in the budget to allow for periods of leave. Or you might have just the right amount for four-and-a-half salaries. But not only do you need the financial resources (the money), you also need the human resources (the right number of suitably qualified people to fill the posts). It is all very well having the money for four-and-a-half medical posts, but if you can only get three people willing to do the full-time posts and one to do the half-time posts, you have only four people to make up what we said earlier should be a 1:5 rota.

Now, assuming you have the money and the people, and your only task is to organise the rota, the decisions that I raised earlier still have to be made. If you have a 1:5, does that mean that you will rotate or that each person will always do a given day of the week (eg. Dr Blogg's SHO is always on-call on Mondays)? And who will make that decision? Will it be you on your own? Or will the five of you get together and decide together? If there is a disagreement, how will you all resolve it? Suppose two of your colleagues want split weekends (Saturday on one weekend and Sunday on another) and two want two-day weekends? You may end up with a casting vote, but then whichever you choose, the colleagues whose preferences you voted against may well be angry with you — even if your vote was not more valuable than any other. You could, of course, guard against this by insisting on a secret ballot. But then your losing colleagues might accuse you of rigging the result. All very silly, you might think — but that is politics.

The point is that there are a number of ways of deciding, none of which are perfect, and none of which will leave everybody who is affected by the decision happy.

Moreover, we have only considered the open ways in which decisions are made. There are all sorts of things that people can do covertly to affect the decision. For example, three of the group may have met before the meeting and arranged how they will vote, irrespective of the arguments. Or the person who is lumbered with every Friday night on-call may catch colds (or have migraines, or learn that their ageing great-grandmother has just died) just a little too frequently on Friday afternoons, thereby 'reluctantly' having to ask a colleague to cover — a favour that is not always returned. In such a way, Dr Smith may be rostered to be on-call for twenty-six Friday nights in a six-month period; but if, after annual leave, study leave, and emergency absences, Dr Smith has only done a total of two Friday nights on-call, he or she has, in effect, altered the decision as to who will be on-call on Friday night — even if the alteration is only that it will not be Dr Smith (without clarifying who it **will** be).

Politics involves a number of strategies to get what you want. Some are agreed as legitimate (such as a fair vote) and some as non-legitimate (such as bullying and intimidation, or repeatedly letting the others down). While the choice of tactic will affect how people are seen by their colleagues — as nice or nasty, trustworthy or unreliable — the outcome is what matters. As we saw, if Dr Smith ends up only doing two Friday nights out of twenty-six, then in effect he or she has not done Friday nights any more than a colleague who was not rostered for Friday night, but who covered on two occasions.

For doctors, many of whom have an idealistic view of wanting to help people, the use of foul means might seem particularly undesirable. But you must remember that in politics, it is the outcome that matters, not the means. Is it better to use underhand tactics and end up getting a better outcome for your patients (eg. a new ward) or to use only fair tactics and find that your patients are deprived of the treatment they need? That is not a rhetorical question, since winning by underhand methods on one occasion may be followed by several losses on future occasions, as people are no longer willing to support you.

I should make it clear that I (like you, perhaps) do not approve of such politics. But the fact that many of us find the political process unappealing does not alter its existence or its reality. For people who would rather not focus on politics, it is wise nevertheless to accept it and to try to work with the process rather than against it. To try to act as though the political process does not exist is wishful thinking, and will lead such a person to have no chance of influencing the outcome.

For those of us who wish to be 'moral and decent', we do have the option of trying to restrict ourselves to those political activities that are open and above-board, such as making appropriate professional relationships (a network), using 'fairness' as a preferred principle of decision-making, and so on.

More broadly, politics occurs in any situation where a group of people make decisions that affect them all, such as in:

- families
- institutions (schools, NHS, golf clubs)
- businesses/companies
- large social groupings (national and local governments, etc).

In any of these situations, resources (money, people, accommodation, other necessary goods) are limited and choices have to be made. A family consisting of a mother, a father and two children may have Saturday free from the obligations of work and school. That day is only twenty-four hours long. They may decide to spend the day together, but the amount of time will be reduced by the amount of time that the last person takes to get out of bed (if it is 11.00 am, then the available time is already reduced to thirteen hours). If it is 8.00 am, then the family has three more hours to spend together, but the person who would have slept in has three hours' less sleep. This is an example of 'opportunity cost'. When we make a decision to do something, we are also accepting that we are losing the opportunity to do something else. When the family is ready to be together, they may decide to go to a museum between the hours of 1.00 pm and 4.00 pm. In doing so, they are losing the opportunity to go and see a matinee that starts at 3.00 pm. In such a situation, there is no 'right' thing to do; there are only decisions to be made.

There are a variety of methods to make decisions — on the basis of principle (eg. a vote); behaviour of one or more members (eg. one family member sleeping in, one worker calling in sick, being abusive or childish, having a tantrum or bullying); or on the basis of power. The decision can be made by one individual; by the whole group (depending on the size of the group); by a few of the group (eg. the parents, who then impose on their children — or vice-versa!); or sometimes by default (eg. you have the TV on and you simply watch the next programme that follows, not because you have made a conscious decision to do so).

Power is the ability to influence the decision. It is not always the case that one person has all the power; often several people involved in the decision-making process have a limited amount of power, which they may all be exercising in different ways.

You should bear in mind that the political process, which occurs in all groups, happens for every decision that has to be made, whether large or small. The family has to decide on its day off whether to go to the seaside, a museum, the theatre, or to stay at home. But it also has to decide how much milk it will buy, which school the children will go to, what colour the walls will be painted, and so on — for every single issue for which a choice must be made.

The NHS is a massive organisation, said to employ in the region of one million people. It covers a wide geographical range (the whole of the UK) and is felt to be 'owned by the people' with funding being taken from general taxation and passed from the Government to the NHS. The number of different people involved in making the NHS work is vast. As well as the doctors, nurses, psychologists, physiotherapists, radiographers, other paramedical staff, porters, cleaners, ward clerks, secretaries, managers and administrators in a wide variety of specialties, along with an army of support staff — estates staff, electricians, plumbers, painters, canteen staff, payroll staff, human resources staff, hospital shop staff, hospital radio staff, volunteers, etc — there are the politicians, journalists, patients and the public, all of whom not only have an interest in the NHS, but also have some degree of power and influence over how it is run, either nationally or locally.

It is not surprising, then, that the plethora of eventual decisions will range from some obviously appropriate ones — such as a patient with appendicitis having his or her appendix removed by a competent surgeon – to some obviously absurd ones – such as patients being asked to attend hospital on a given day, only to be told that their operation has been cancelled, and for this process to occur to a given individual on more than one occasion.

But the NHS is not the only healthcare provider in the country. Apart from the private hospitals and organisations ('private medical practice'), opticians, dentists, chiropractors, homoeopaths and other practitioners of complementary medicine offer people services aimed at some form of health improvement. These are paid for out of the savings and income that individuals possess after Government taxation, but still represent a form of choice over expenditure of the country's overall income (its Gross National Product [GNP]).

In looking at the politics of medicine, the broadest questions involve:

⌘ How we pay for treatment – privately or state funded?
⌘ Who gets treatment – given that demand for medical treatment exceeds supply not only of money, but also of staff skilled in the relevant disciplines?

The private sector provides treatment in accordance with the patient's ability to fund that treatment, either from his own pocket or via an insurance mechanism. With finance as the basis of treatment, it may be believed that sometimes this affects medical decision-making. For example, a study has shown that in Brazil more Caesarian sections are done in the private sector than in the state sector (Potter *et al*, 2001). The authors question whether this can be accounted for entirely by medical need.

Conversely, the public sector uses a larger pot, restricted by the Government. Although it is a substantial amount, it cannot meet the demand (and clinical need) for treatment. Choices therefore have to be made — by people who may not be affected by the consequences of those choices. If someone who is deciding opts to put more money into orthopaedics than into renal medicine, fewer people will be able to have renal dialysis and more to have total hip replacements. The orthopaedic surgeon and the renal physician will have different views on this decision, and it will usually be difficult to know whether such a decision would be 'right' or 'wrong'. The State of Oregon in the USA attempted to address this in a democratic manner in an experiment a few years ago (Ham, 1998) in which the public decided which 500 medical conditions would be funded, whereas anything else would not be. Unsurprisingly, when the voting had taken place, the results announced and the system of funding started, people who had conditions 501 and 502 (for which funding had been abolished) shouted long and loud — with the result that the experiment was stopped.

A government wanting to address the problem of the limited supply of publicly funded treatment has two options:

⌘ Increase available treatment.
⌘ Reduce demand for treatment or deny patients treatment.

A government has several ways of increasing the availability of treatment:

⌘ Employ more doctors, nurses and other medical staff.
⌘ Pay for more medical equipment (X-ray machines, MRI scanners, etc).
⌘ Get others to pay for treatment:
   ❖   charges for non-nursing care, etc
   ❖   charities funding treatment out of donations.

It also has several ways that it can reduce demand:

⌘ Operate waiting lists:
   ❖   a person who stays on a waiting list and dies before obtaining treatment has, in effect, been denied treatment, while the appearance of being offered treatment is preserved.
⌘ Reduce time in hospital:
   ❖   where technological advances make this possible, this is valid; but sometimes it seems that patients are discharged before their clinical condition has improved sufficiently for them not to need hospital care.
⌘ Rationing.
⌘ Limit options available to the cheapest ones, irrespective of quality (eg. generic drugs).
⌘ Delay building new hospitals.
⌘ Use committees to make decisions.
⌘ Reply slowly to letters.
⌘ Delay purchasing decisions.
⌘ Dismiss 'experts'.
⌘ Deny that a person is ill (or, in public, deny that there is a problem).
⌘ Deny condition as illness (eg. smoking).
⌘ Blame others for not providing.

Some of these methods may seem unacceptable, but when politicians use any of these methods successfully, they are only doing so with the implied consent of the public to tolerate such behaviour. (For an excellent dramatised account of this process, read Ibsen's *An Enemy of the People*.)

Since the inception of the NHS, there has always been discontent at the way that decisions about resource allocation have been made. If you have a condition for which you receive timely and appropriate treatment, you are delighted. If you are denied treatment, you are angered. From the point of view of the clinician, it is the patients for whom resources are lacking who occupy you, and it is easy to overlook the excellent treatment that a good number of patients do get.

But the current perception is that things are a little worse now than previously, as decisions seem to be taken to meet the goals of the professional politicians rather than on medical grounds. Many in the medical profession feel that the priority is to do what is needed to get the Government re-elected (ie. reduce waiting lists) rather than to ensure that the most ill patients get the treatment their conditions require. If the NHS is to return to its former glory (assuming that this is not just a nostalgic illusion), clinical need must return as the basis of resource allocation. If this does not occur, it will be important for those clinicians who continue to work in the NHS to recognise the constraints within which they work.

Stigma

All patients are not created equal. Some people have fashionable diseases, others dirty diseases. Whether a disease is trendy or not varies over time. And the fashion extends to the view of their doctors.

Cardiology and neurology have long been trendy diseases. The best doctors go into their specialties. And as for cardiac surgery — that is the bee's knees. So, if you've got a good *bona fide* heart problem, or maybe a nice neurological illness, you're okay.

HIV is a curious one. Initially, it was a disease to be shunned, with offensive descriptions of it as a 'gay plague'. Although a viral illness, its sexual transmission permitted bigots to feel that their criticism of people with HIV and AIDS was a legitimate expression of homophobia. But thanks to a fair degree of lobbying by the gay community (amongst others), huge progress was made. An explosion of research led to the antiretroviral drugs and a wave of sympathy led to the provision of high levels of benefit in the UK and good medical facilities in which patients could be seen. Indeed, it led a consultant surgeon to ask if the patients she saw with breast cancer could not have similarly high-quality facilities.

But as the homosexual community started to practice safe sex, the disease started to be spread by heterosexual transmission. The World Health Organization (WHO) has expressed significant concern about the damage it is doing. In some countries, large proportions of the people of working class age are being affected, with huge damage to the economy. Children are losing parents and old people have no-one to look after them. But for the bigot, it is all right, as the countries being affected are mainly those in Africa. Homophobic sentiment is replaced by racist sentiment.

But HIV is a virus. Smallpox is a virus. Measles is a virus. Both the latter viruses can kill, albeit less frequently (especially if smallpox has, as WHO claim, been eradicated from the world). But their transmission is not sexual, so people don't feel able to get on their moral high-horses. Of course, as a doctor, I am not interested in moralising about how the infection is spread (and I hope that you, as a doctor, feel the same). It is only relevant insasmuch as it allows us methods of prevention. Condoms prevent the spread of HIV; they do not prevent the spread of measles. But in terms of treatment, I treat the person and the illness, however acquired.

Mental illnesses have never been trendy. The public has a distorted view of mental illnesses and the people who suffer them. This is strange, since mental illness is so common that there can be few people, if any adult at all, in the country who has not come across someone with a major mental illness. For many, they will have direct involvement with the mentally ill person.

The Royal College of Psychiatrists, as part of its campaign against stigma and mental illness, writes on its website:

> *... people with these conditions often attract fear, hostility and disapproval rather than compassion, support and understanding. Such reactions not only cause them to feel isolated and unhappy, but may also prevent them obtaining effective help and treatment.*

(Royal College of Psychiatrists website, www.rcpsych.ac.uk)

Stigma (which literally means 'a mark', as in 'the mark of Cain') involves viewing another person as second-class, or of lower value. Patients with mental illness may well be regarded as second-class citizens. Sometimes, so are the doctors who treat them. Psychiatrists can feel that members of the other Royal Colleges do not regard them as 'proper' doctors. This is odd, because psychiatrists have had some training in physical medicine (cardiology, pharmacology, surgery, etc) and have done jobs, even if only at houseman (intern) level, in medicine and surgery. But general physicians and surgeons have little or no experience or knowledge of psychiatry, yet presume to pontificate on it.

This would not matter, but 'popular' diseases receive better funding than stigmatised diseases. The history of state provision for people with mental health problems does not exactly cover any country with glory. When the worst excesses of the asylums were finally acknowledged, the response was to close them, without retaining those features that were beneficial, and which were lost in the underfunded drive to 'community care' in the UK. Among those who care for the mentally ill, there is a lot of re-inventing the wheel going on, just to make up for aspects of the asylums that were not replaced as the politicians rushed to sell off the site (some of which had become valuable. For example, in London, the asylums were originally built at some distance from the town. With the expansion of the city to the M25, these sites were by then within the main suburbs of London, and represented a valuable asset when the decisions were taken about the provision of care for the mentally ill).

How can we respond to the stigmatisation of patients with mental disorders — and of their doctors? We should start (as always) with ourselves. What are the lay attitudes that we have inadvertently brought with us to the practice of psychiatry? Do we talk about people with a diagnosis of schizophrenia, or do we label them 'schizophrenics', as though the adjective covered the whole of the patient's being? (Do we talk about 'measlics' or 'COADics'?) And do we believe that the mental disorders are illnesses, or just naughty behaviour? Do we think that they are simply the result of bad behaviour, either on the part of the patient or his family (now, or in the past, such as when we find a history of child abuse)?

There is a welter of clinical and research information that makes it clear that the mental disorders are illnesses. (And don't forget that the chapter on mental disorders in the 10th edition of the *International Classification of Diseases* is as much a chapter as any other in the book.) But they are not the same as physical diseases. Koch's postulates (three criteria that must be fulfilled before attributing an infectious illness to a pathogenic agent such as a bacterium or virus) do not apply to schizophrenia. But then they don't apply to a broken hip either. And we don't deny that the surgical treatment of a broken hip is not real medicine, just because it occurred in a young aggressive biker who came off the vehicle at ninety miles per hour.

No, if you have read the research literature, there is no doubt that the mental disorders meet all the criteria you could want for an illness. There are clear biological correlates to schizophrenia, bipolar disorder and obsessive-compulsive disorder. And for the addictive disorders and eating disorders, there is much to confirm that they are complex neurological responses to adverse circumstances. You may wish to claim that they are socially induced illnesses, and there may be much truth in this. But then hypertension is a response to a chronic western diet and nobody refuses to see high blood pressure as worthy of medical attention.

Perhaps you have been seduced by the erroneous disparagement of psychiatric therapies as 'only talking cures'. But words, wrongly used, can kill. And they can therefore be used to cure and save lives. Constant bullying in the form of name-calling can lead children to kill themselves. The proper use of conversation can help a child to change how he or she thinks about himself or herself. Of course, talk takes time, unlike a pill that you pop in your mouth. I would not wish to disparage pharmacological therapies either. But it is easy to reject psychotherapy if you don't want to spend the money (and the NHS certainly doesn't). The psychiatric disorders are serious illnesses, of a different form to physical illnesses, but susceptible to diagnosis and treatment by skilled practitioners.

So face up to the stigma that ignorant lay people (including non-psychiatric doctors and nurses) bring to bear regarding mental disorders. As a psychiatrist, you should hold your head high, secure in the knowledge that the job that you do is as valuable as that done by medical colleagues in other disciplines.

Having clarified where you stand regarding your own practice of psychiatry, look at your patients as people suffering from serious medical disorders. They are disadvantaged enough by their illnesses. Someone with schizophrenia will never hold a job commanding the same sort of salary as a lawyer or businessman who has had a heart bypass after a heart attack. Feel appropriate sympathy and concern for your patients — and expect the same from your non-psychiatric medical, nursing and paramedical colleagues, the managers working in the healthcare system, your friends in your personal life, and the general public.

Structures of provision of psychiatric care

One of the most salient features of severe mental illness is the way it interferes with the person's ability to get and keep a job. That is not to say that everyone with a mental illness is unable to work – far from it – but more than other branches of medicine, the majority of patients do not have the means to pay for treatment privately. The burden falls mainly on the State. There is a small but significant private sector, and the newspapers are full of stories of celebrities who are admitted to one of the Priory hospitals. But, in general, many people are treated by the State (*Figure 5.1*).

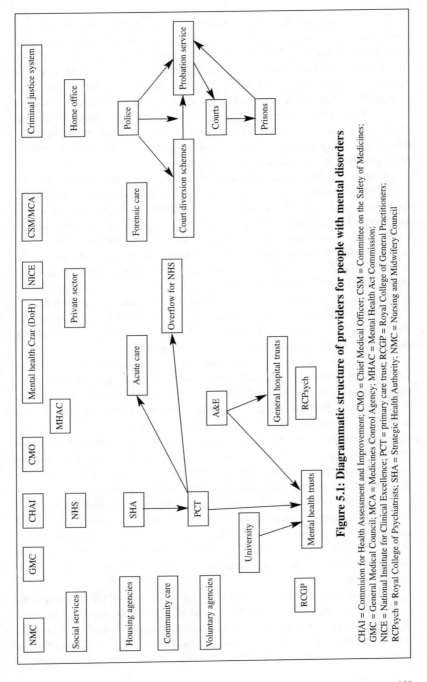

Figure 5.1: Diagrammatic structure of providers for people with mental disorders

CHAI = Commision for Health Assessment and Improvement; CMO = Chief Medical Officer; CSM = Committee on the Safety of Medicines; GMC = General Medical Council; MCA = Medicines Control Agency; MHAC = Mental Health Act Commission; NICE = National Institute for Clinical Excellence; PCT = primary care trust; RCGP = Royal College of General Practitioners; RCPsych = Royal College of Psychiatrists; SHA = Strategic Health Authority; NMC = Nursing and Midwifery Council

Since the 1990s, the funding of health care in the NHS has involved a separation of the administrators who apply for the funds for treatment ('purchasers') and the wide variety of clinicians who provide the treatment ('providers'). The intention is that purchasers consider which services are needed by the residents of the geographical area for which they are responsible. There should be a number of different providers — some of the traditional type, others who might not have offered treatment for NHS funds previously — who would compete for contracts. The intention is that this would encourage innovative types of practice and incline people to offer services at the most competitive price.

In practice, there are too few people with the requisite skills to offer effective treatment to make the market mechanisms work effectively, and the excess of demand for treatment over the funds available means that in areas where treatment is particularly labour-intensive (as in psychiatry), there is only so much reduction of cost that can be put into the system before quality of service is inevitably reduced. Thus, the reduction in the number of beds available in the mental health trusts, a trend which was evident even in the 1960s, has exceeded any putative technical advances in patient care that would lead to a reduction in bed use. And with the Government, through strategic health authorities and primary care trust as the only purchaser of NHS services, the lack of competition between purchasers means that services cannot be fully funded.

Clinicians come across the result of such funding deficits daily; administrators who make the decisions without seeing patients cope with the funding deficit in the political ways of denial, blaming the service providers and using fashion rather than clinical criteria as the basis of service purchase. Hard though it may seem, this description of the perversions caused by the funding gap to the purchase of services is not meant to be read cynically: it is only by understanding the process that the clinician can stand back and ignore what cannot be changed (and not take the absurdities of the middle-ranking administrator to heart).

The result of the process is that a few competing providers attempt to meet clinical need from an inadequate pot. There is no serious chance of the amount of money being used for state health care to be increased in real terms. Contracts are often full of unrealistic hopes and expectations, but as they are often short-term (two years is typical) it is not possible to plan for the long-term.

The structure that is currently in place is that many GPs treat a large number of people with less severe mental illness. Some psychiatrists have difficulty acknowledging stress as a reputable mental disorder, but GPs are managing on a daily basis patients with a variety of mild psychiatric illnesses, including those whose psychosomatic symptoms can be attributed to stress, not organic pathology; mild to moderately severe depressive illnesses; a variety of life difficulties, including marital problems, unemployment, domestic violence; and the chronic management of major mental illnesses that are clinically stable (though the symptoms have not gone into remission), such as schizophrenia and bipolar disorder. The majority of patients with mental illnesses are treated in primary care.

Patients who are considered to require specialist services in secondary care are mainly offered 'community care'. In this, community mental health teams act as the point of entry, and the patient may be initially assessed by any of the multidisciplinary team of doctors, nurses, social workers, psychologists, occupational therapists and any other clinical worker who is employed. The community mental health team (CMHT) is now the focus of care, and attempts are made to limit hospital admission by using the CMHT in the first instance, unless an emergency prompts direct admission to hospital.

Conceptually, there has been a change in the view of the use of the acute general psychiatric ward over the last fifty years. Previously, people who had one episode of mental illness had the possibility of being admitted to mental hospital, never to come out again. Now, however, acute episodes of mental illness are regarded as justifying a brief admission to a hospital ward — lasting a matter of weeks — before the patient returns to the community as the episode resolves.

Specialist psychiatric services are provided by mental health trusts, who have various divisions, according to the age groupings of child psychiatry, adult psychiatry and old-age psychiatry (*Chapter 2*), with subspecialties such as eating disorders, psychotherapy and addiction being fitted in. For many trusts, the demands of forensic psychiatry are great enough to warrant a separate division.

The trust structure is that there is a board responsible for its running, modelled on the structure of a public company in the business sector. There is a chief executive; a few non-executive directors; a medical director; a director of nursing; a finance director; a human resources director; and other directors as felt locally necessary. In the case of the doctors, there is a line-management approach. The medical director is supported by clinical directors — consultants who take on the managerial role for their own section of the trust, and who are responsible for the line-management of all the doctors (consultants or otherwise) in that section. The days of the entirely autonomous consultant are over.

The needs of psychiatric patients, however, are greater than the provision of care for an acute exacerbation of a chronic condition. Social care, including attention to housing and benefits, is required, and although the focus of this book is on the medical aspects, the absence of adequate social care is no less problematic for patients as any lack of medical care. One of the problems for people working in the NHS is the frequent constant re-organisation of the structures that has gone on over many years. Although health and social-service structures are drawn separately in *Figure 5.1*, the next re-organisation will involve the combination of health and social services in new health and social care trusts.

Those who do not manage to obtain housing often have to sleep rough. Agencies such as St Mungo's and Shelter, charities that aim to help the homeless, run hostels where the staff gain a working understanding of how to support people with mental illness.

The lack of social care is highlighted by the large proportion of people in prison who have mental illnesses. Some have attributed this to lack of beds in the NHS, but whatever the reality, a number of people with mental illnesses are picked up by the police. There are, of course, provisions in the Mental Health Act (1983; Section 136) for people to be brought by the police to hospitals and for courts to sentence people who have committed offences to hospital rather than to prison. However, the system is far from perfect, and psychiatric care often has to be offered by prison medical officers, with even fewer resources than in the NHS.

Although people with mental illness suffer a great deal of stigma, there are now groups who look out for their welfare. The views of service users are now required to be considered by trusts, and many have patient advocates. Although the relationship between trust senior executives and advocacy agencies is in its infancy, and trust and goodwill is not always established, it is encouraging that there is an acknowledgement by the system that it really ought to listen to the views of those whom it professes to wish to help.

Patient advocates look to the welfare of individuals, but there are also organisations for the patients that have a varying mixture of self-help and campaigning. SANE, the National Schizophrenia Fellowship (recently renamed Rethink) and MIND are three organisations that have been particularly vocal on behalf of their members, and they are also able, to varying degrees, to offer practical advice to patients and their relatives about living with mental disorders.

Clinical governance

So. You finally made it through training and you are doing the job with gusto. But do you provide a good service? Do you treat your patients properly?

How dare you ask, I hear you reply. I am not implying that you do not do your best. Nor am I denying that you help a good number of people. But no-one is perfect. Everyone makes mistakes. And we are all affected by our surroundings. If the hospital has no beds, how can you admit anyone? Or if you try to admit someone to a twenty-eight-bedded ward when there are already forty patients on the books, are you providing a good standard of care? Or, more accurately, is the **hospital** (of which you are just an employee) providing a good standard of care?

Clinical governance is the process whereby clinicians look at what they do and consider whether they could do it even better. (Audit, discussed earlier in the book, is one element of clinical governance.) They also look at where they are making mistakes, or why people are making complaints.

If we think about it further, in a more positive light, this is the way that good doctors take medicine forward. They are always thinking about what they are doing and asking themselves if they could do it better. Could the operation be done with a smaller incision? If the heart is a mechanical object, why can it not be transferred between people? If chlorpromazine treats the symptoms of psychosis, is there another drug similar to it that treats psychosis just as effectively — but without the side-effects?

The additional point for clinical governance is that, although it requires people to look at individual practice, it does so within the context of the performance of the whole organisation (the trust). And clinical governance has now been introduced as a concept throughout the NHS. If you work in the NHS, it is a duty. If you do not, it is still a requirement of the General Medical Council that you do the best you can for your patients.

What are the points we all have to consider? They fall into three categories:

1. What are we doing and can we do it better?
2. What are the things that could go wrong if we don't take some form of action (ie. what are the risks)?
3. What are we doing badly that we need to correct?

For the first category, we can look at our practice by simply asking — where are we, and are we happy with what we find? In other words, you start by thinking what you are trying to achieve. If we were to take schizophrenia, we would find it easy to agree that it is the role of the doctor to try to relieve the symptoms of psychosis. You could look at whether you are doing that. You might find it a strange question, but if you looked back over the last six months at all the new patients who came to your service — whom you diagnosed as having schizophrenia and started on neuroleptics — you might find that not all of them had had their psychotic symptoms relieved several months later. How many did you treat and how many had their symptoms relieved? Was it 40% , 60% or 90%? If the figure was low, why was that? Was there something that you could have done to get a larger proportion of the patients better? If so, are you going to bring it into your practice now? Are you going to check again in (say) six months' time to see if you got a higher figure into remission?

The more astute of you will have noticed that I have just described doing an audit of your outcome in the treatment of schizophrenia. But that audit is not strange, weird or wonderful. It is, in fact, very straightforward. At baseline, what was the proportion of patients who got better in the previous six months? You looked in your files, added up the total you saw, the number that did improve, and the number that did not improve. And then, after making some change, you did the same calculation again.

What was it that made the difference? The idealist researcher will tell you that you cannot know if it was your intervention that made the difference or some other factor. True — but if you make an intervention and find no change, then you can deduce that the change had no effect, so you still learn.

The factors that could have made the difference vary widely. It could be that you prescribed too low a dose of neuroleptic. It could be that the patients did not take the medication (but did not tell you). It could be that the pharmacies locally did not stock the neuroleptic you chose. It may have been the fact that the patients could not afford the prescription charge (and did not know that they did not have to pay). The important issue in this brief and selective list of possible causes is that they are different types of cause. In respect of the dose of neuroleptic, that is within your control – you can look at the doses and see what you are prescribing. But you cannot control whether the pharmacies stock the neuroleptic you prescribe, especially if this is not brought to your attention. (There may be good reasons for why this might happen.) But the different types of reason show how a system can fail: if the doctor prescribes what the pharmacy does not stock, because of a restricted list that the doctor did not know about, the effect is that the patient does not get the medication. And although we have chosen an obvious example (in the case of ensuring that neuroleptics are effective in your patients' care), you should ideally review every aspect of what you do with, and for, patients. At least, you should think about it as much as you can in the time available for clinical governance.

To make your guesses as to why some patients did not do as well as others, despite similar treatment, you would base it on two things — a look at how your organisation works, and what research tells you. In the latter case, the research literature may answer a relevant question. If it does not, you may wish to attempt to answer it yourself, if you have the time and resources (especially money and research workers).

What you cannot do is know what it is like to be on the receiving end of treatment. Even if you happen to have suffered from the same condition (now in remission, allowing you to work), you cannot know the experience of a patient at that time in your hospital. The only way you will find out is if you ask him or her. So do so. The way that the organisations are learning to do this is by having patient advocates — people whose job it is to describe the patients' experiences, and make appropriate criticisms. That is why user involvement is such an important issue at present. Equally, you must not swing from one end of the spectrum to the other — you should not go from the assumption that whatever the doctor says is right to whatever the patient says is right. In a proper conversation, the views of both the doctor and the patient are synthesised to produce a way forward with which both are happy.

I have described the processes of audit and user involvement in personal terms. However, since the concept of a doctor 'running the show' has been almost completely replaced (particularly for workers in the NHS and private organisations), and because doctors realise that they are each no more than one member of a multidisciplinary team, it is actually the team and the organisation (the trust or hospital) that has the responsibility to perform the audit and to involve users. In this respect, we see a difference between medical audit (the review of the medical component of the delivery of care to a patient) and clinical audit (the review of the whole team's provision of care to a patient). Although one always wants to be reviewing one's own practice, as there are so many people involved in the delivery of care, clinical audit is more important and I understand that it will be sufficient for a doctor involved in clinical audit to have completed this aspect of the appraisal and revalidation procedure.

From the patient's point of view, this also makes more sense. If the team's system for offering appointments fails (and this may well be delegated to an administrator), then however good the doctors and nurses in the team are, the patient does not get the care required. The clinical team involves everyone who will have anything to do with a patient receiving care, including the receptionists and secretaries. It is now the responsibility of the team manager, not the consultant, to see that clinical audit and user involvement occur.

As well as reviewing past practice and incorporating the views of service users into the way the team works, it is important that the team not only maintains its skills, but also improves them. In practice, this means that every member of the team ensures that their knowledge is constantly being increased and that skills are constantly being practiced. The process of 'continuing professional development' is crucial. It involves looking at what you know and what you need to know, taking steps to fill in the gaps.

Of course, good doctors always do this in the form of reading journals and attending professional conferences. But the knowledge base is so great that not only do you need to know about the technical information for the practice of your discipline, you also need to know about a whole variety of other issues too: such as IT; presentation skills; management; teaching; politics — many of which are introduced in this book. Having established what those gaps are, it is your responsibility to ensure that the organisation knows of those gaps so that it can help you fill them. (The process of informing the organisation of the gaps is that of appraisal, discussed in *Chapter 2*.)

The team manager also needs to ensure that everyone is doing their job properly. You cannot know whether you are doing your job properly if you do not know what your job is. You have to ensure that you have a job description. From that, and in conjunction with your manager, you have to devise the goals that you should achieve in given periods of time. Again, this is the process of appraisal, which involves a regular look at how people are performing in respect of their clearly defined goals. For example, you may be asked to carry out a clinic in a given session of the week, but have no time allocated to writing letters to GPs and others after the clinic. You have to discuss with the manager when you can write those letters and — given the limitation on time available — what you will drop. It is now up to the manager to ensure that the task that is to be left out of your full timetable, by mutual consent, is done by someone else.

After ensuring that people in the system are functioning at their optimum, there will still be uncertainties that have to be considered to avoid an adverse outcome. In other words, it involves an understanding and assessment of the risks a patient's condition presents, so that efforts can be made to manage those risks. Managing risks does not mean that adverse events never occur. It means recognising the possibilities and taking steps that reduce the likelihood that such an event will happen.

For example, psychiatric patients will often become distressed and violence is a rare, but real, possibility. The risk of someone being harmed can be reduced if members of staff have other people that they can call on easily if a dangerous situation arises. For example, on a home visit to a patient, it is usual for mental health professionals to visit in pairs if the patient is unknown to the service or is known to have a greater potential for violence. It does not mean that a staff member in such a situation will never get assaulted — occasionally, regrettably, it happens (even when there are two staff). And when the politicians talk about risk-management as though it were a guarantee that nothing adverse would ever happen, one needs to remind oneself of the reality that the presence of the second staff member reduces the risk of assault, but does not abolish it.

The obvious risks in psychiatry involve the potential for suicide or violence, but risk involves the whole continuum of care. There may be risk factors for relapse, such as refusal to continue to accept depot medication, or stress and high-expressed emotion in the family. There may be risk factors to health in a more general sense, such as in the case of poor housing or poor social support. And there may be aggravating factors, such as alcohol or drug use, which may increase the likelihood of a given patient becoming more psychotic or acting out violent feelings or hallucinations. The major risk factors differ between the different types of psychiatric illness and each department may draw up its own check list of risk factors. But as long as that list has been drawn up and considered by the team for each patient (and appropriate steps put in place), the risks will be minimised.

In every group of people, professional or otherwise, there are always a few bad apples. When the processes of evaluation of doctors (appraisal, revalidation, etc) are fully implemented, it may be expected to confirm what most people believe at present — that most doctors are doing a pretty good job. As are most nurses, social workers, psychologists, secretaries, receptionists, etc.

But that does not mean that we should not attempt to identify those few doctors whose practice is poor. In a small minority of this group, it will not be possible to remedy their practice and they will have to be prevented from continuing to offer medical services. But for the majority of those whose practice is poor, there may be good reasons why they are not performing properly. They may have chronic illnesses (especially addictions); they may have adverse social circumstances; they may have felt that they had to take on far more than they could possibly be expected to cope with (such as in the case of a GP who feels unable to refuse to take more patients onto his or her full list because he or she is the only doctor in the area); they may not have had time to keep up with medical progress; they may not have a good bedside manner; or there may be a number of reasons that are amenable to change. In many of these cases, support from the employing organisation can help the doctor improve significantly, and the NHS gains from retaining the services of an experienced doctor.

But it is preferable to identify doctors who are performing at less than their optimum at as early a stage as possible, and to take steps to remedy the situation when they can be more easily done. Of course, no-one likes to feel that they are being criticised, but it is easier to approach if the manager has some form of objective data. If a doctor (or any other member of staff, for that matter) is performing poorly, it is likely that people will notice. Both their patients and their work colleagues are likely to start talking about the difficulties they have and, if they continue or are serious enough, will make complaints. If a doctor becomes the subject of a number of complaints, this can be brought to his or her attention, and a discussion can be initiated.

A well-meaning doctor who is being prevented from adequate practice by external circumstances will welcome a sympathetic review of the obstacles in his or her way, as long as it is backed up by serious provision of support (eg. the offer of an additional colleague — but this must be followed up by being put into practice). Some doctors will not feel able to accept the criticisms and will deny them, suggesting reasons or justifications for each that may (or may not) be spurious. It may be that these doctors will require a more disciplinarian approach.

As with all these matters, it is better to use objective rather than subjective evidence: with a doctor who has difficulty acknowledging criticism, it is possible for the manager to say that the number of complaints against this doctor are so many and that it exceeds the average of his or her colleagues by such and such an amount. The manager can then say that he or she expects the number of complaints over the next period of time to be reduced and that he or she will help the doctor to achieve this. It will be up to the doctor to make the necessary changes: if the rate of complaint continues, then disciplinary action, including dismissal, can ensue. The NHS has now created an agency, the National Clinical Assessment Agency, to assist doctors whose performance needs modification. Its services can be invoked when local attempts have not resolved the matter.

Clinical governance is therefore a duty for all individual staff to ensure their knowledge base (CPD); evaluate and review their practice (clinical audit); take on board what patients say (user involvement); assess the risks inherent in the patient's clinical condition (risk management); and address poor performance. It is backed up by external review, both from internal managers (such as the clinical director) with the use of assessment and appraisal, and from external reviewers such as the General Medical Council, with the process of revalidation.

But clinical governance applies also to organisations. The NHS has set a series of standards that trusts and other NHS providers must meet (eg. the National Service Framework [NSF] for Mental Health). Numerous external agencies are able to come in to inspect that they are meeting those standards — the Commission for Health Improvement, The Royal Colleges, and other official bodies. The National Institute for Clinical Excellence (NICE) provides a formal evidence-based assessment of a number of the technologies employed in the NHS, and comments on the appropriateness of their use.

Trusts are required to ensure that there is accountability for good performance, so that a complaint can be made to the right person. The trust must make note of the complaints made against it, and what it has done in response to the complaints that have been upheld on investigation.

Trusts must ensure that their staff are of the right calibre, that they are doing the right jobs, and that they know what they need to. The NHS has provided much information, and the development of KA24, through which NHS staff have internet access to major peer-reviewed journals and other sources of good-quality medical information, is a significant step forward in assisting NHS staff to access up-to-date medical and other clinical knowledge.

Trusts ensure that their staff know the parameters of their organisation by the dissemination of important policy and procedure documents. Trusts must listen to the views of service users, both informally and by formal mechanisms, such as the use of patient advocacy.

Trusts also have to ensure that they have risk-management procedures in place and be aware of problems, particularly by the recording of adverse clinical events and the instituting of internal inquiries into serious untoward events. The trust must also require its staff to co-operate with national initiatives to assess adverse events, such as the Confidential Suicide Inquiry.

This is, of course, just a brief overview of clinical governance. It is important that individuals and organisations constantly review every little step that is relevant. The detail is mind-boggling, and so has not been considered here. Examples would include whether patients can physically get into the buildings (Is there wheelchair access? How might a blind person get round a building where the signs are all written, but not in Braille?); or whether, if it would help to have written advice to patients how to take their medications, the advice should be available in the patient's own first language; or whether it is acceptable to wait two days for a phlebotomist to take an ill patient's blood.

What is important, especially when one is at the earlier stages of a specialist career, is that the burdens imposed on all by the demands of clinical governance are not seen as irrelevant or meaningless. It may take many years before many of the vast number of issues that clinical governance raises are fully addressed, but the improvements that are seen will be real.

Further sources of help

Below is a list of further sources of help. Please note that this list is not intended to be comprehensive, but to give you some initial places to look

The best way to approach any problem is to ask the people around you — ask several, and when they give you differing answers, sort out what is common to them all. Ask any expert you can, especially friends who will give you pointers. Go to bookshops and libraries (general ones for non-medical matters) as there will almost certainly be something helpful. Search the internet. Remember: what may seem a new problem for you is almost certainly one that has cropped up numerous times before.

I Planning a career

Suggested reading

ICD-10 Classification of Mental and Behavioural Disorders. Clinical Descriptions and Diagnostic Guidelines. 10th edn. World Health Organization, Geneva

American Psychiatric Association (1994) Diagnostic and Statistical Manual of Mental Disorders. 4th edn (DSM-IV). American Psychiatric Association, Washington

Gray C (2000) Making career decisions yourself. *Br Med J* **320**(7238): S2: 2–3 (http://www.bmj.com/cgi/content/full/320/7238/S2-7238)

2 Getting a training

Introductory texts

Brown D, Pedder J, Bateman A (2000) *Introduction to Psychotherapy: An Outline of Psychodynamic Principles and Practice*. Routledge, London

Cohen RM (2000) *The Presentations of Clinical Psychiatry*. Quay Books, MA Healthcare Limited, Dinton, Salisbury

Cookson J, Taylor D, Katona C (2002) *Use of Drugs in Psychiatry*. 5th edn. Gaskell, London

Goldberg D, ed (2000) *Maudsley Handbook of Practical Psychiatry*. OUP, Oxford

Hamilton M (1985) *Fish's Clinical Psychopathology*. John Wright, Bristol

Leff J, Isaacs A (1981) *Psychiatric Examination in Clinical Practice*. Blackwell Science, Oxford

Sims A (2002) *Symptoms in the Mind*. Baillière Tindall, Edinburgh

Part-time working

Gibson H (1997) Are part time doctors better doctors? *Br Med J* **315**: 2

Jones R, Crawley H (1997) Job sharing. *Br Med J* **314**: 2

MacDonald R (2003) Flexible and family friendly working in the NHS. *Br Med J* **327**: 59s–60

Morrell J, Roberts A (1995) How to do it: make an application for flexible (part time) training. *Br Med J* **311**: 242–4

Assessment and appraisal

The Department of Health does not have one specific site for appraisal – to find out what is most appropriate for you, look at its website (www.doh.gov.uk) and then search the site under 'appraisal'.

Anderson, Elliott (2003) Lessons learnt during the appraisal process. *Hospital Doctor* **3**

Audit: see clinical governance below

Examinations

Curriculum for basic specialist training and the MRCPsych examination (2001) Council Report 95. Under review. (www.rcpsych.ac.uk/ publications/cr/cr95.htm)

Personal accounts of mental illness

As well as being academically competent, it is important that you understand what the patient is experiencing if you are going to be most effective as a doctor. Personal accounts of illness help greatly. National newspapers often have stories of what it is like to be mentally ill, described by sufferers. It is useful to look at them, as they are in the public domain and you can discuss what has been written.

Suggested reading

Anonymous (1982) Personal view [alcoholism]. *Br Med J* **285**: 130

Anonymous (1990) Reflections after manic depressive psychosis. *Br Med J* **300**: 1597

Anonymous (2003) The loneliness of the alcoholic doctor. *Br Med J* **327**: s78

De Quincey T (1821) *Confessions of an English Opium Eater*. Penguin Popular Classics, London

Freedman BJ (1974) The subjective experience of perceptual and cognitive disturbances in schizophrenia. *Arch Gen Psychiatry* **30**: 333–40

Haw C (1990) Coming out [experience of depression]. *Br Med J* DETAILS

Lloyd G (1982). I am an alcoholic. *Br Med J* **285**: 785-6

Rapoport J (1990) *The Boy Who Couldn't Stop Washing* [OCD]. Collins, London

Wigoder D (1987) *Images of Destruction* [autobiography of manic depressive illness]. Routledge, Kegan Paul, London

There are numerous descriptions and depictions in various forms of the media – plays, films, particularly, too numerous to mention beyond:

- *A Beautiful Mind* (film and book; schizophrenia)
- *Iris* (film and book; Alzheimer's disease)
- *Rain Man* (film and book; autism)
- *As Good As It Gets* (film; OCD)

Note that all such depictions will inevitably be distortions to meet the needs of the drama.

3 Putting your career in the context of the rest of your life

Personal finance, getting a mortgage

For information about personal finance, you can start by looking at the personal finance pages in the daily newspapers. Also the BBC business website (http://news.bbc.co.uk/1/hi/business) currently has introductory information. You should be careful of advertisements and think about seeking advice from an independent financial advisor. You should consider only buying products from companies regulated by the Financial Services Authority. Should you find you need debt counselling, you could start with the Citizens Advice Bureaux (www.nacab.org.uk).

Getting married

Relate (www.relate.org.uk) deals with couples, married or unmarried, who have got into difficulties with their relationships.

Having children

You are likely to find it helpful to have some guides. Two popular ones are:

Biddulph S (1998) The Secret of Happy Children. Thorsons, London
Leach P (1988) *Baby & Child — From Birth to Age 5*. Penguin, London

Each person has to find a book that suits them. They are widely available in bookshops. You may be interested (as a parent and psychiatrist) in:

Bettelheim B (1987) *A Good Enough Parent*. Pan Books, London

Divorce

Relate: see getting married above

Working when chronically ill or with a disability

International Labour Organisation (ILO) (2002) Managing disability in the workplace. ILO, Geneva. (www.ilo.org/public/english/employment /skills/disability/download/code.pdf)

Demanding relatives

www.voluntarysectoronline.org.uk contains links to a number of websites that deal with the elderly and their illnesses, such as the Alzheimer's Society.

Bereavements

Public information is available at:
http://www.rcpsych.ac.uk/ info/bereav.
htm www.crusebereavementcare.org.uk

4 Management skills

Bhugra D, Burns A, eds (1995) *Management for Psychiatrists*. 2nd edn. Gaskell, London

The Jerwood Medical Education Resource Centre of the Royal College of Physicians has produced detailed reading lists on the following topics:

- management for doctors (Oct, 2002)
- consultant appraisal (Sept, 2003)
- educational supervision (Sept, 2003)
- assessment (Sept, 2003).

Time management

McGuire R (2003) Successful time management. *Br Med J* **327**: S117

Griffiths M (2003). Tips on creating time for yourself. *Br Med J* **327**: s086

Assertiveness

Lindsay C (2002) Being assertive. *Br Med J* **324**: s027

Working with other disciplines

Health Care Team Effectiveness Project (2002). *Team Working and Effectiveness in Health Care*. Aston Business School, Aston University (http://research.abs.aston.ac.uk).

Presentation skills

McGuire R (2002) Tips on making the most of conferences. *Br Med J* **325**: S31

5 Psychiatry in its social context

Introduction to economics and politics

If you wish to look at these subjects in more depth, you could buy any standard textbook available in high-street or academic bookshops (they are standard 'A' level subjects).

Ham C (1998) Retracing the Oregon trail: the experience of rationing and the
    Oregon health plan. *Br Med J* **316**: 1965-9
Potter JE, Berquó E, Perpétuo IHO *et al* (2001) Unwanted caesarean sections among
public and private patients in Brazil: prospective study. *Br Med J* **323**: 1155-8

Stigma

Information on the RCPsych campaign against stigma can be found at:
www.rcpsych.ac.uk/campaigns/cminds/index.htm

Clinical governance

For information about how the NHS plans to introduce governance and related
documents, see the Department of Health Clinical Governance website
(www.doh.gov.uk/clinicalgovernance).